Wel... ...Good and Faithful Mommy

An honest and encouraging book every mom will love
and every mom needs.

Marlene Bagnull

Director, Colorado and Philadelphia Christian Writers Conference
Author, *Write His Answer*

"Precious mom"—those are the words Megan Breedlove
uses to address the "good and faithful mommy" who reads this
book. The very heart of this book is to understand how precious we
are. Until we truly comprehend how we are fearfully and
wonderfully made and treasured by the One True God, we are not
going to escape the never-ending hamster wheel of people-pleasing,
seeking fulfillment and affirmation from others, and just trying
to attain some invisible goal of being the "great mom."
With poignancy and candor, Megan leads the reader through
her message of hope, joy and freedom. Her teaching is grounded in
the Word of God and inspired by experience and humility.
The more you open your heart to the lessons presented,
the more your life will be transformed.

Amy Eichler, Ph.D.

Mom, Stepmom, Child and Family Psychologist

Jesus loves you, and Megan wants to make sure you know it!
He loves you with a love so deep, so complete and so fulfilling that
if you seek to know Him, you cannot help but feel satisfied. This
book came at a deeply painful time in my life, and it
was such a monumental blessing to be reminded that I have a
perfect parent in Jesus who will love me and show me the way
as a busy mom and wife. In spite of my shortcomings, He is
faithful to help me overcome them. You, too, will be reminded of
the precious love, healing and rest that Jesus makes available to
His children as you raise yours.

Tonya Sakowicz

Professional Nanny

If you are a mom, Megan Breedlove knows your story. Her warmth and easy humor pour into each word in an intimate and tender way. She honestly bears her heart and gently exposes the deep thoughts and needs that most moms keep hidden. If you feel a little lonely—maybe a bit unappreciated—Megan's insights will help you see mothering through new eyes and discover true fulfillment. Well done!

Lori Wildenberg

Co-founder, 1 Corinthians 13 Parenting
Licensed Parent and Family Educator,
Co-author, *Empowered Parents*

I enjoyed Megan's last book so much, so when she asked me to read this book, I was honored and excited. Reading *Well Done Good and Faithful Mommy*, I must say it felt as if Megan pegged me straight on. I was the young mom of two beautiful daughters but always felt as if I were not a good mom. I can remember saying I felt I worked for my family, instead of being part of it. I had a list of things to do everyday and never got them finished . . . I must not be a good mom. I never seemed to get the laundry washed and put away . . . I must not be a good mom. I never felt my family—or God—was pleased with my performance as a wife and mother. As I began to read this book, I figured out I still feel that way. I thank Megan for sharing this with me—it is freeing to know others struggle with the same things I do and a wonder to be reminded that God loves us where we are, not where we are going. Thank you, Megan, for writing a book that lifts us out of who we think we are and teaches us who God says we are.

Susan Wood

Director, Hope Center for Autism

Well Done Good and Faithful Mommy

Finding Fulfillment as a Mom-on-the-Go

Megan Breedlove
Author of *Manna for Moms*

Regal

For more information and
special offers from Regal Books, email us at
subscribe@regalbooks.com

Published by Regal
From Gospel Light
Ventura, California, U.S.A.
www.regalbooks.com
Printed in the U.S.A.

Breedlove, Megan.
Well done good and faithful mommy : finding fulfillment as a
mom-on-the-go / Megan Breedlove.
pages cm
Includes bibliographical references and index.
ISBN 978-0-8307-6634-5 (trade paper : alk. paper)
1. Mothers—Religious life. I. Title.
BV4529.18.B735 2013
248.8'431—dc23
2012051448

Rights for publishing this book outside the U.S.A. or in non-English languages are
administered by Gospel Light Worldwide, an international not-for-profit ministry.
For additional information, please visit www.glww.org, email info@glww.org, or write to
Gospel Light Worldwide, 1957 Eastman Avenue, Ventura, CA 93003, U.S.A.

To order copies of this book and other Regal products in bulk quantities,
please contact us at 1-800-446-7735.

FOR EVERY MOM
WHO HAS EVER WONDERED
IF ANYONE SEES OR CARES.
WHAT YOU DO MATTERS,
AND YOU MATTER.

AND TO THE ONE WHO
MATTERS MOST OF ALL.
I LOVE YOU.

Contents

Foreword

By Suzanne Eller

Not too long ago, our family got slammed by a virus over Christmas. One grandbaby landed in the hospital. Three more, all under the age of 30 months, were coughing and cranky and seriously ill. Then it hit the adults.

For the next two weeks we banded together as a family to make it through the crisis. One morning I held 13-month-old Jane on my hip and stirred steaming oatmeal on the back burner. Every time I tried to put Jane down she cried and held on to my sweatpants, begging to be picked back up.

I finally gave up, and we ate Cheerios and blueberries.

We were both snotty, sick and needed a nap. I wasn't sure if I had brushed my teeth that morning, but I was certain I needed a shower. As I held my precious grandbaby, praying for the other in the hospital, I knew that if I just hung on, things would get better.

That's why I am so grateful for the book, *Well Done, Good and Faithful Mommy*. Parenting is one of the most beautiful privileges we have as women, but some days it's just plain tough. You might be sleep deprived as you nurse every three hours, or a master coordinator as you schedule extracurricular activities. You cook. You carpool. You clean. You correct. You cheer.

And then someone asks you, "What do you do all day?"

The answer is that you are transforming the heart of a child. You're pouring in encouragement and advice, and you are shaping a human being into a person of character and faith. What you do not only matters; it's also crucial.

During our recent battle with the virus, it brought me back to the time I had three babies under the age of 19 months (twins!). I loved my babies, and raising them was a gift, but it was chaotic and hectic and wonderful all at the same time. There were definitely days that I needed to hear those words, "Well done, good and faithful mommy."

As those three children grew up and became new parents themselves, they have asked me for advice. They have trusted me often with my precious grandbabies. They have let me into the moments when parenting is hard and they need a break, and they call often to share the fun and exciting and silly moments.

I can't wait to place this book in my daughters' and daughter-in-love's hands as they take care of the daily to-dos of being a mom. I just know they will benefit as Megan comes alongside in the trenches to share practical encouragement, humor and raw honesty as moms all over the nation work hard at the most important job of all.

Suzanne Eller
Proverbs 31 Ministries speaker, *Encouragement Café* radio co-host, *Moms Together* host, and author of *The Unburdened Heart* and *The Mom I Want to Be: Rising Above Your Past to Give Your Kids a Great Future.*

Acknowledgments

With gratitude, I acknowledge the following for their contributions to the writing of this book:

My husband, Phil. Without your willingness to take on the lion's share of the childcare and housework duties at times so I could write, this book would never have happened. Thank you for believing in me not only as a writer but also as a mom.

My children, Ellie, Kenny, Lindsey, Jessica and Timmy. You are the best five kids I could ever ask for. I have learned and received so much from you. Thank you for being willing to share Mommy's attention when Mommy was writing. Wait until you hear the post-book celebration Mommy has planned for all of us!

All the precious moms who shared their stories with me. Some quotes made it directly into this book; unfortunately, there wasn't room to use them all. But each of you helped me learn and grow. Any ministry God brings about through this book is partly yours.

My editor, Kim Bangs. I love what you've done with this project. You have a God-given ability to see what's there and tweak it in just the right way so it'll best express what God wants it to say to everyone who reads it. I love knowing that someone who truly loves God was shepherding this book.

All of you who prayed for me as I worked on this book. Some of you, I've met in person; others, I've only met online. But all of you approached the throne of grace on my behalf. There is no greater thing you could have done for me. This book is God's answer to your prayers. Any ministry He brings from it is partly yours as well.

Introduction

I think God wanted me to write this book because He knew I needed the message too.

Had you asked me before I had children, however, I would have told you I didn't need any special encouragement. You see, in my pre-child days, I knew exactly how being a parent was going to go. And it was going to be easy. *After all*, I thought, *how hard can this parenting thing be? They're little; I'm big. They're inexperienced; I've read lots of books on parenting. This will be a slam dunk.*

It's okay; you can laugh. I laugh at how naïve I was then. I shake my head at how unaware I was of what parenting really entails. Sure, I knew I'd have to change lots of diapers and maybe even lose sleep every now and then (though I really didn't think it would be that often). I knew I'd have to work hard. But I was certain that my passion to be a mom, and my excellent parenting skills, would be more than sufficient.

It never occurred to me back then that as a mom, I might feel unappreciated.

Before I had children, I had a career that I loved. I enjoyed the work and at times even reveled in it. As an added bonus, I received appreciation and thanks on a daily basis from the people I dealt with.

It never occurred to me that as a mom, things would be different.

Sometimes, I don't enjoy the work. Who really enjoys cleaning up vomit or refereeing squabbles about things that don't really matter, and trying to figure out whom (if anyone) to discipline? Or—and this actually happened to me recently—getting urine out of the couch cushions because somebody didn't want to stop watching TV and go potty?

And sometimes—okay, the vast majority of the time—I don't receive lots of thanks and appreciation, at least not in the way I would like to receive it. Nobody ever says, "Thank you for washing my shirt after I smeared jelly all over it," or "You're really awesome at cleaning French fries out of the back seat of the van." It's not that I have to be thanked for every little thing; it's just that I want

to feel appreciated. I want to feel that what I do is noticed and valued, not taken for granted.

• •

At the beginning, motherhood was a lot harder than I expected.
My sweet son was so wonderful right from the beginning.
He slept pretty well, ate well and was an overall happy baby;
so I couldn't figure out why I was feeling so inept. My friend finally
explained it to me. I am a very driven person. Most everything in
life has come easy to me. I always attributed that to God's grace
and blessings as well as to being a good steward of those blessings.
But my friend hit the nail on the head. I had expected it to be
as easy as everything else, and as every mother knows,
motherhood isn't easy for anyone. —Angela A.

• •

Every mom I know wants the same. We all long to feel that
someone notices what we do. That they're grateful for it. That
what we do *matters*.

Many moms don't feel that way. We might *know* it in our
heads, but we don't *feel* it in our hearts. And that's where we long
to feel a deep assurance that we are significant and that what we
do is significant.

We crave the security of knowing that the people we love notice, and that they care about what we do for them. And by exten-
sion, care about us. Because if what we provide doesn't matter,
then do *we* really matter?

Precious mom, you matter far more than you realize, and
that's the message of this book: What you do matters. You are significant, and so is the ministry you pour out upon your loved ones,
day in and day out, 365 days per year, in sickness and in health.

Throughout the course of this book, we'll look together at
how we know this is true, what difference it makes and what that
means for us in our daily lives. We'll learn that we really are appreciated, and we'll learn how to get our "appreciation cup" filled all
the time.

We'll get plenty of prayer time too. Don't feel intimidated by this. If you don't know how to pray, or you feel a little awkward, be assured that there's no one "right" way to do it. You just jump right in and tell God what's on your mind. He knows how to hold up His end of the conversation.

Sound good to you? It sounds wonderful to me. So let's get started by looking at what happens when our ideals about motherhood run smack-dab into reality.

Going Deeper

Do you ever struggle with feeling unappreciated? If so, take time right now to pray and tell Jesus how you feel. He cares, and He wants to hear from you. Tell Him you can't wait to hear His solution to your need.

While its communicated frequently about how appreciative they are it is difficult when just moments later the room is messy again, or a chore asked to be done is met w/ a huff -- or not completed.

It feels as thogh the appreciation was false as thier end of the bargin never was goning to be held up.

1

Ideals vs. Reality

Last night, I had an awesome night of sleep. I went to bed at 10:00 p.m. and slept in until 10:30 a.m., when I woke to breakfast in bed being served by my husband and immaculately groomed children. I lounged against my pillows, drinking my coffee and listening to the kids tell me how much they love me. They even asked what they could do for me today!

Okay, not really. I don't get that kind of morning very often. Actually, never.

My mornings are usually more like this: I sleep in until 6:15, when the baby wakes up for the third time, wanting to be nursed. As I haul myself out of bed from beside my sleeping husband, my seven-year-old meets me at the door of my room, saying, "Good morning. Will you make me breakfast?" I agree to make him breakfast after I nurse the baby, and I sit down with my littlest one, only to have another child wander sleepy-eyed into the room and say, "Mommy, I peed in my bed." Before I can even say, "Go put on clean clothes," I hear a familiar sound. Yep, the cat is barfing again.

The first scenario makes most of us laugh because it's so far from reality; the second makes us nod and say, "Been there." Rarely is the perfect morning we'd *like* to have the morning we actually *get*. Ideals crash up against reality on a daily basis, and reality usually wins.

When this happens on a regular basis, it's easy to get discouraged. Sure, we know we can't have things our way all the time, but shouldn't we get what we want *sometimes*? In our minds and hearts we answer yes, but then we see our ideals getting crushed repeatedly, and we get discouraged. We begin to feel unfulfilled and empty.

 Motherhood is hard. One of the ways it's hardest is in learning to die to self—to go without what we want so that others can have what they need. That's not only because, as human beings, we instinctively seek our own good; it's also because we've linked others' meeting our needs with our ability to feel fulfilled. In other words, if people are meeting our needs adequately, we feel fulfilled. If they're not, we feel empty.

• •

Every morning, I wake up with the notion that I am going to do what I have on the schedule—or at least what I would like to do—including school time, playtime, cleaning, and so on. But somehow it just NEVER works out the way I want. For example, right now I am going to have to get off the computer, because my son has informed me that my two-year-old got the Cheerios and dumped them underneath our indoor play slide. —Lyv C.

• •

Our dilemma becomes even more complicated due to the fact that one of our primary needs as moms is to feel appreciated. It's not that we expect to be thanked for every little thing; it's just that we want to know that what we do matters to the people for whom we do it. If our family doesn't show their appreciation for us, we feel taken for granted. Invisible. Unappreciated. Unfulfilled. Because, apparently, what we do doesn't matter.

We'd love to hear our husband thank us for being the mother of his children or for the job we do raising them. But most men (understandably, as we will see in the next chapter) don't think of saying things like this, and we take their silence to mean they don't appreciate us.

We'd be ecstatic to hear our children express gratitude for disciplining them, encouraging them and taking them to Chuck E. Cheese without complaining about how it makes our ears ring for an hour afterward. But it's highly improbable that that's ever going to happen, at least not until they're adults. Seems like the best we can hope for, for now, is that they remember to say thank you out of politeness, even if there's no conscious appreciation behind it.

So we settle for what we realistically *can* have instead of what we *wish* we could have. But too much settling, for too little, for too long, leads to discouragement.

That's because, when we decide to become moms, we don't anticipate the emotional toll that motherhood will exact from us. We know being a mom will entail a lot of work, but we assume it will mainly consist of diaper changes, laundry and carpools. We're prepared for the middle-of-the-night feedings, the trips to the doctor (or the ER) and the endless rounds of Candy Land. What most of us are completely unprepared for is the emotional cost of pouring our hearts and lives into other human beings without receiving as much in return.

• •

The times I cherished the most with my kids were our times spent in the car. Any topic was fair game for conversation, and I quickly learned that one never knew when a child would feel like opening up about inner feelings, or have major questions. One day, when my youngest daughter, Martha, was six, we were heading home in the car, and apparently she had heard the gospel presented recently. She asked me, "Mama, do people have to ask Jesus into their hearts to go to heaven?" "Yes," I replied. "If a person asks Jesus into his or her heart, and asks Him to forgive his or her sins, then yes, that person will go to heaven when he or she dies." "Will I go to heaven when I die?" Martha asked. "Well, honey, I don't know, but I hope so. Have you asked Jesus into your heart and asked Him to forgive your sins?" "No, I don't think so." "Well, would you like to pray now about that?" I asked. "No, not now," she replied. "Okay. Well, you think about it, and maybe when we get home." So we got home and went into her room, and she confessed her sins to the Lord that very day and received Jesus into her heart. My heart was thrilled! —Cindi M.

• •

We expect motherhood to be one long road of endless bliss as we cuddle with our children on the couch and read Bible stories.

Granted, those moments do happen, but they are *moments*. They are not nearly as constant as we envision.

. . . .

The thing that surprises me most about being a mother is how much it affects every single part of your life. Once you're a mother, you can no longer buy an article of clothing or even go to the bathroom without thinking of your child. —Kristen L.

. . . .

Most of the time, we live somewhere in what I call the "lack"—the sometimes bleak terrain between what we *have* and what we *wish for*. We feel as if we're running on empty, mothering on willpower instead of real fuel.

Then we feel guilty. We tell ourselves we shouldn't need all that affirmation. After all, we're Christians, right? We're supposed to serve without any thought of getting anything in return, aren't we? (Or so we think.)

We try not to let our discouragement steal our joy, but it does. We make every effort to pull ourselves up by our own bootstraps, emotionally speaking, but that doesn't work. We wonder if something is wrong with us, or maybe with our faith.

King David wrote, "I am weary with my moaning; every night I flood my bed with tears; I drench my couch with my weeping" (Ps. 6:6). For most of us, it isn't quite that bad, though it can get that way at times. Still, the constant, nagging discouragement and emptiness remain.

Have you been there? Have you experienced the disconnect between the way things are and the way you'd like them to be? Have you felt the discontent in your soul and wondered what you could possibly do about it, or if anything *can* be done about it?

I have. I bet you have too. We both know it's painful to live in the no-mom's-land between ideals and reality.

Of course we have romantic images of motherhood and ideas about what it will be like, and there's nothing wrong with that. After all, God doesn't want us to begin this incredible venture by focusing on all the things that could go wrong. Ideals are fine. In fact, they can even help us during the hard times by giving us something to hope for.

It's also not wrong to be disappointed when life doesn't go the way we desire. Jesus understands how we feel. Over and over in the Scriptures, He expressed grief or distress when things didn't go right (though of course His idea of "right" is always accurate; ours sometimes needs a little—or a lot of—fine-tuning). He wept for Jerusalem, who refused to turn to God, crying out, "O Jerusalem, Jerusalem, the city that kills the prophets and stones those who are sent to it! How often would I have gathered your children together as a hen gathers her brood under her wings, and you were not willing!" (Matt. 23:37).

We have another example in the Gospel of Mark: "When he went ashore he saw a great crowd, and he had compassion on them, because they were like sheep without a shepherd. And he began to teach them many things" (Mark 6:34). Compassion is not a feeling you have when everything is going well. Jesus had compassion on the people because they had been harassed by the religious establishment and were helpless to adequately bear the burdens placed upon them.

In the Old Testament, God the Father reveals that He is moved by the sufferings of His people. When He called to Moses at the burning bush, He said, "And now the cry of the Israelites has reached me, and I have seen the way the Egyptians are oppressing them" (Exod. 3:9, *NIV*).

He is moved when things do not turn out as they should. Yet we also know that He is still content and satisfied.

We, on the other hand, struggle. For us, being contented in the face of discouragement is hard.

In order to come to a place where we can be at rest even when our circumstances are not pleasing, the first thing we must do is realize that living in between the "what is" and the "what we wish for" is not the problem, even though we think it is. When we begin to feel discouraged or unhappy, we tend to expend our emotional energy on trying to change our circumstances so that our negative feelings will go away. We'd rather change the circumstances that produce our feelings than accept that we have to change our feelings in the midst of our circumstances.

As a young mom, I was no exception. It had been a difficult transition for me from working outside the home to becoming a stay-at-home mom. Both my husband and I agreed that I should make the transition, and I wanted to, but it was hard. I loved my career, where I regularly (as in, every day) received praise and thanks from those I dealt with. As a stay-at-home mom, however, I almost never received either praise or thanks. There was little-to-no interaction with other adults, unless you counted the cashier at the grocery store. I felt lonely and empty.

• •

Sometimes I miss the companionship from the workplace, but I remind myself how blessed I am to be able to stay at home with my kids. They're only little for so long. I need to cherish every moment. —Amy L.

• •

So, not liking those feelings, I did what I could to change my circumstances. I made play dates for my kids even though they weren't old enough to care. I took frequent shopping trips so I'd have a reason to be out in public. I joined the YMCA and taught a Spanish class for children. In fact, I was so lonely one time that I participated in a group aerobics class I didn't care about just to have people to be with.

There wasn't anything intrinsically wrong with my doing those things. It's fine to belong to the Y or go to Wal-Mart. It's also reasonable to consider whether changing some of your circumstances might help. But it's a mistake to pin all your emotional hopes on changed circumstances. I would have been far better served—and a far better servant—had I dealt directly with my feelings about motherhood rather than trying to avoid them by busying myself with other activities to distract myself.

We'll talk in this book about some legitimate ways to make things easier on ourselves. But there's simply no way to make things so perfect that we never have to feel any unpleasant or negative emotions. That won't happen until we reach heaven (where it will then be done *for* us abundantly more than we can ask or imagine).

Until then, we have to learn how to live down here in the less-than-perfect. How to live well and fully, even in less-than-fully-desirable circumstances. Be assured that this is possible, precious mom. The details of your life will not be fully perfect. But you can live with soul-deep satisfaction even in the midst of circumstances you'd change if you could.

That's what this book is about. Together, we'll explore how living this way works and what it looks like. But first, we need to look further at the issue of appreciation and at the people from whom a mom usually expects to receive it.

Going Deeper

Do you have any negative feelings about motherhood? Be honest with yourself. Then be honest with Jesus. Talk to Him about how you feel and what you would like to be different.

The added load to my plate. While for the most part I feel supported by John I have a desire for more.

When I do want to do a mom event he makes me feel bad b/c he doesn't do that w/ dads.

2

Why Don't They Appreciate Me?

Kids have a way of humbling you.

Not too long after my first book was published, my oldest daughter, Ellie (then eight years old), overheard a phone conversation between my husband and me. Someone had purchased a book through my website and requested to have the book autographed. Ellie listened thoughtfully until the conversation was finished, then said, "Mommy? I have a question."

"What is it?" I said.

"Why do people want you to sign your book if you're not famous?" Ellie asked.

Then there was the time I was giving an unexpected radio interview and called my husband to let him know that I would be on the air soon. As my husband tells it, after he got off the phone with me, he asked the kids, "Hey, want to come listen to Mommy on the radio?"

"Um, no thanks," they said. "Can we watch a movie instead?"

If I depended on my kids' affirmation in order to feel fulfilled as a writer, well, I wouldn't feel very fulfilled. They're polite and express happiness for me when I'm published, or something similar happens, but they don't *get* it, which is understandable. After all, they're young children.

So if I want to feel encouraged enough to continue as a writer, I have to look elsewhere. I can't depend on my kids to make me feel fulfilled—nor should I.

Yet inside of me there is an "appreciation cup" that I long to have filled to the brim. You have one too. Some days, it's filled to the top; other days, there's nothing but dregs in the bottom. The people we depend on don't always fill our cup like we want them to.

Megan Breedlove

Husbands? Not always. Children? Not usually. Family and friends? Maybe sometimes. Society? Not likely.

But instead of bashing these four groups for not doing their job, let's look at the reasons why they fail. If we're going to depend on these people, we need to know going in that they're not going to be able to fully meet our affirmation need, and why.

Your Husband

When I was engaged to the man who is now my husband, I thought we were fully prepared for marriage. My husband-to-be had a degree in marriage and family counseling from Southwestern Baptist Theological Seminary; so did I. In the course of his training, he'd read plenty of books on marriage; throughout the years, I, being an avid reader, had read even more. So we had degrees, we had books and we had love. What more could we possibly need?

Yeah, I'm laughing too, because I know now what I didn't know then: Even hundreds of books and a whole lot of love aren't enough to enable a couple to understand each other perfectly. There will still be times of misunderstanding. There will be times when you think you understand each other, only to find out later that you've been wrong for a while now. Sometimes, there will be just plain confusion.

Why? Not only because you're a woman and he's a man, but because you are two different human beings, and no two humans on this planet will understand each other and meet each other's needs without ever making a mistake.

- -

I'm sure my husband appreciates me, but he doesn't always show it. He tells me I'm a good mom, but it's usually when I'm crying because I think my child hates me. — Kristen L.

- -

You probably already know this, but men don't always understand women. Why not? Because they're insensitive? No, because men and women are so different.

That's actually a good thing. God made men and women different not only so the process of procreation could take place, but also so that each gender would be suited to its role in life. Your husband's God-given nature inclines him to want to be a leader and to protect and provide for you. Your God-given nature prompts you to be a nurturer and to make a home for your family.

With such differences between the genders, is it any wonder that your husband sometimes fails to understand you simply because he is a man? For that matter, you, being a woman, don't always understand him. When a woman says something like, "I don't understand how he just doesn't *get* it," she is actually revealing a lack of understanding of her spouse that is as profound as his lack of understanding of her.

Because your husband is a man, he will sometimes fail to understand you. And if he doesn't fully grasp your need for appreciation and how you would like it to be shown, he can't fill your cup. It's not because he won't, but because he can't. Even if your husband is the most wonderful guy in the world, he is still limited in his understanding of you, just as you are in your understanding of him.

Not only that, but he probably has other things on his mind. If your husband takes seriously his role as provider, his job will take up a lot of his mental and emotional energy. Your husband is wired to care deeply about succeeding in his work, which is actually good for you and your children. But it means that at times, work will occupy his thoughts when you wish your needs were occupying his thoughts.

The apostle Paul wrote, "If anyone does not provide for his relatives, and especially for his immediate family, he has denied the faith and is worse than an unbeliever" (1 Tim. 5:8, *NIV*). Sounds like a pretty hefty responsibility to have, and most husbands are very aware of their accountability in this area.

Your husband may also be a fan of a sports team or a hobby, such as fishing. Naturally, these leisure pursuits require mental energy too. That's because a man is made to desire to succeed at *everything*—which means it matters to him when his team wins, or whether he catches a fish. Again, this desire to succeed is actually a good thing for you and your children. You wouldn't want your husband not to care about succeeding in life.

Another reason your husband might not meet your need for appreciation is because he's tired of being nagged about it. (Ouch.) When you repeatedly nag your husband to do something for you instead of approaching him lovingly and respectfully, you give him the impression that you believe he can't succeed in pleasing you on his own. Most often, when a man is committed to a situation (marriage) in which he believes he can't succeed, he will withdraw. Instead of trying to please you when it won't do any good, he may just try to get out of your way.

Solomon wrote, "A quarrelsome wife is like a constant dripping" (Prov. 19:13, *NIV*). No wonder our husbands avoid us when we nag them. Nobody likes to hear the unrelenting sound of a leaky faucet. *Drip. Drip. Drip.* It's annoying just to think about it, which is how our husbands feel when they think about being nagged by us.

Then again, maybe your husband does have a fairly good understanding of your need for appreciation. That is, he knows that you need and desire to feel appreciated. He may just not know how to make you feel this way. Men understand what makes another man feel appreciated, and usually that's far different from what makes a woman feel appreciated. Your husband would know what to do to show a buddy appreciation, but he might honestly be at a loss to know what to do for you.

That's not because he doesn't care. It's because he simply isn't certain what the right answer is. So rather than try and fail, he may choose not to try. Or he may try, get it wrong and decide not to try anymore if he can't get it right anyway. Our husbands are not mind readers. "He should know without my having to tell him" doesn't work out too well in real life. After all, we women don't always know exactly what we want. How can we expect our husbands always to know?

Even when we tell our husbands what we want, it sometimes takes time to sink in. That's because learning something new usually takes time. It's no surprise that our husbands may need several chances to get it right. Ladies, can we just be satisfied that at least they're trying, and give them a little grace?

There's one more factor to consider that influences your husband's ability to meet your need for appreciation—to fill your appreciation cup—and that is that he has an appreciation cup of his own that needs filling. Your husband may be frantically trying to get his own cup filled, which doesn't leave him as much time as you would like for filling your cup.

Maybe this is an area where you can help him. How much time do you spend trying to fill his cup as opposed to demanding that he fill yours? See, that's the way marriage is designed to work: Each spouse pours into the other from the fullness he or she has received from God and from the other. It's beautiful when it works that way—the way God designed it.

In fact, it's a command. Paul wrote to the Thessalonians, commanding them to "encourage one another and build each other up, just as in fact you are doing" (1 Thess. 5:11, *NIV*). That command still applies to us today. Paul didn't say, "Nag each other if your spouse isn't doing a good enough job to build you up." No, he made it unconditional by making it a command. Encourage your husband and build him up, no matter what he does or doesn't do for you.

You just might be surprised to find that when you fill his cup, he has more energy available (and more desire!) to fill yours.

Your husband may, at times, be legitimately unable to fill your appreciation cup. At other times, he may not fill the cup because of sin. But even when he tries, he is unable to fill it perfectly, because he is a mere human being. Tragically, when a wife feels that her husband doesn't do a sufficient job of filling her appreciation cup, she sometimes turns to her children to meet her need.

Your Children

Whether it's because her husband doesn't fill her cup, because she feels that her children "owe" her, or for some other reason, a woman who turns to her children to give her all the appreciation she craves is turning to people who can't possibly do what she wants.

Children, by their very nature, are immature. They're still trying to figure out how to be a person, much less how to finesse the finer points of social interaction. They just don't always realize when they should be appreciative. It simply doesn't occur to them.

We're working on this right now in our family. My husband and I want our children to say thank you when someone does something nice for them, such as holding the door or jumping up to get them a snack. We have taught them that God wants us to be thankful for His blessings, which He sometimes sends through other people. We've also taught them that when they don't say thank you, the person blessing them may not know they're thankful. That's why it's important to speak our gratitude verbally.

Despite our teaching, they sometimes still forget. We've explored various strategies to get them to say thank you without having to be reminded, but we haven't been completely successful yet. Our kids still have difficulties with this issue. That's understandable, because they are still young.

If it's that difficult for children to remember to express appreciation for concrete things (going to McDonald's, receiving a gift), how much more difficult is it for them to express appreciation for less tangible benefits such as endurance or patience on your part? Kids just don't think like that. They don't realize that your being patient with them, teaching them to get dressed or even playing with them is work.

I remember a time when Ellie was six or seven and I was having a hard and wearisome day. Being the perceptive child that she is, she asked me if something was wrong. "No, sweetheart," I said. "It's just that parenting is hard work sometimes."

"What's so hard about it?" she asked.

It was a great question, from her perspective. Children simply don't realize the effort it takes to get up in the middle of the night when you're bone tired, or to patiently remind them to do something when you've already told them a million times. There-fore, since they don't realize you're doing something special, they don't realize they should be thankful.

• •

We've all had mornings like Christy S.'s. That Tuesday morning, nothing went right. Christy was trying to get ready for work, as well as get her kids ready for school so they could all leave the house at the same time. She kept telling them to hurry, but they were still taking too long. Finally, Christy and the kids left the house. But then, "I get halfway down the long driveway, and my oldest has forgotten her bag. And I turn around—I'm mad—and I'm about to say something I shouldn't, and I have to take a deep breath and remember that she's eight, and she's not intentionally trying to make them late for school and me late for work."

• •

We moms don't always understand this. *I know I did something for them,* we think to ourselves. *It should be obvious to them too.* But it isn't. They're kids. They won't fully realize what we've done for them until they have children of their own.

Sometimes, when a mom doesn't understand her children's lack of expressed gratitude, she tries to guilt them into speaking words of thanks (though she may not realize she's using guilt as a motivator). She may say things such as, "After all I've done for you, this is how you treat me?" or "I'm the only one who ever does anything around here." Children quickly learn that when mom says something like that, they had better say "thank you," and they had better be quick about it. But they still don't really understand why they should be thankful, because they can't grasp the magnitude of what Mom has done for them.

In reality, you wouldn't want it any other way. You don't truly want your children to understand all that you are doing for them, because that would require that they know the alternative of *not* having those things done for them.

Children who have grown up in homes where they weren't truly loved, where patience and sacrifice were nonexistent or came at a high price, *do* understand. They know what an incredibly valuable gift it is when an adult shows patience with them, puts the child's needs before his or her own and consistently shows love to the child. But their understanding came at a price. They were first denied what they needed and deserved.

I think you'd rather have your children fail to appreciate you sometimes than know just how much they should appreciate you because they've been scarred in the past.

Friends and Family

Your friends and family may not appreciate what you do as a mom either, especially if they don't have children of their own.

I remember a conversation my sister and I had four or five years ago. At the time, she didn't have children (though now she has a daughter). She was a career woman, and I was a stay-at-home mom. Despite these differences, we were close. Perhaps that's why it didn't bother me when she cautiously said, "Meg, I have a question to ask you."

"Shoot," I replied.

"I don't mean for this to sound wrong, but—what is it you do all day, anyway?"

I paused and thought about it. "Well," I said, "I fed the kids breakfast and lunch . . . I played with them . . . I did some laundry . . . uh, I guess that's about it."

"Oh," she said.

I wasn't surprised that Kristen didn't sound impressed. Listening to myself, I wasn't impressed either.

That's because a mom's daily accomplishments usually don't sound like all that big a deal, especially to people who aren't parents or who spend their days dealing with large sums of money or important clients. And if those accomplishments don't sound impressive, there's no need to express affirmation or appreciation because of them.

Kristen would respond differently to my answer now. Actually, after having a daughter, she'd never ask the question in the first place. She now knows that even when there isn't much to show for it, and no list of impressive accomplishments to recite, being a mom does seem to take up all day. She understands that it's a lot harder than it sounds—and this is true whether you are a stay-at-home mom or a mom who receives a salary outside the home.

Other friends and family may have children but still not understand all that you do, for a variety of reasons. Maybe you have special needs children, and they don't. For a time, my son, Kenny, was diagnosable with Asperger's Disorder. During that time, he struggled with some behavioral issues, and we sometimes struggled in knowing how to deal with them. I can't remember anyone ever telling me that I was doing a great job with him (other than his therapists). I can, however, recall a few people who offered their opinion that if I would just discipline him better or spank him more, he wouldn't have the behavioral problems he had.

These people didn't appreciate the work I was doing with Kenny because they couldn't see it. All they could see was his meltdowns, and they figured those were partly my fault. Therefore, in their minds, there was nothing for them to appreciate.

Or maybe your friends and family don't have the same priorities for their children that you have for yours. They might not appreciate what you're doing for your children because they don't understand the importance of it. For example, let's say you have a friend who doesn't take her children to church. She may very well not see the need to affirm you for doing so because she doesn't feel that church is important.

Maybe your friends and family are inwardly focused, trying to keep their own plates all spinning at the same time. As busy as you are, they may very well be that busy too. And when we get busy, we tend to turn inward in an effort to hold it all together.

Or maybe it's simply that they've never received appreciation, so they don't know how to express it. It's hard to give what you have never received. That's one reason Jesus commands us to love one another. He knows that each person needs to feel loved so that he or she can, in turn, demonstrate love to others. When a person hasn't felt appreciated, she will have a hard time showing appreciation. She may not even recognize the need for it since her own need has gone unmet for so long.

There's one final possibility I'd like us to consider: Perhaps your friends and family love you, but they don't understand how much you need them to show it. They may very well have grown up in an undemonstrative home where open affirmation wasn't practiced, at least not regularly. If that's the case, they are unlikely to think about affirming you on a frequent basis.

Whatever the reason, friends and family may be unavailable to you as a significant source of encouragement. When that's the case, it can be painful and discouraging.

Society

Society doesn't do much to affirm moms. In fact, it seems that society is more likely to disparage moms than to uplift them, or even to pit moms against each other in what has come to be known as the Mommy Wars.

If you work outside the home, society tends to value you for the role you fulfill, not for your status as a mom. Working women are expected to be model employees with perfect attendance and an unending supply of energy and creativity, never mind the fact that their toddler was up all night teething. Children simply can't be allowed to interfere with a mom's workplace duties. On the one hand, this is understandable, because businesses must be run well and efficiently to succeed. On the other hand, it's sad, because society thus teaches the mom that she is valued for what she can do for customers or clients rather than for what she does for her own family.

If you are a stay-at-home mom, society doesn't value you, because you aren't contributing anything, at least not the way society sees it. Perhaps you're "wasting" your education so that you can stay home. Maybe you could be "so much more" than what you are. Whatever the messages society sends to a stay-at-home mom, they usually aren't positive. For the most part, the best that stay-at-home moms can usually hope for from society is being ignored. At worst, it's being belittled and scorned.

Sometimes I feel isolated and alone. Teaching was so much a part of me. I loved the interaction with kids and other teachers. My family and my husband's family live hours away. My teacher friends are busy. It's not always easy to get out with a baby, but I'm trying to meet up with people from my church and other friends. —Christi B.

On the other hand, society expresses plenty of appreciation to those whose contributions it deems valuable—actors, sports figures and musicians, to name a few. Not moms. There's no awards show for moms. No mom ever had her name up in lights for her exemplary work with her children. You never see an article in news magazines about moms, unless it's about a mom who also does something for the community. In other words, being a mom won't get you noticed and appreciated by society, but doing something that society deems valuable will.

Then there's the fact that the women who are most admired by society are usually skinny and beautiful. Most of us, especially those of us who have physically borne children, do not have skinny bodies anymore, if we ever did. Yet we are constantly confronted by images of women who are considered beautiful yet who look completely different from us. It's yet another way society devalues moms. It's true, indeed, that while the Lord looks on our heart, man looks on the outward appearance (see 1 Sam. 16:7).

With this lack of appreciation from the sources from which we usually seek it—husbands, children, friends, family and society—it's no wonder that moms have a hard time getting their appreciation cups filled. What makes a mom's position especially difficult, as we will see in the next chapter, is that her inner need for appreciation never goes away, because it is God-given.

Going Deeper

From whom would you like to receive more appreciation? Have there ever been times when someone's lack of appreciation really hurt? Tell Jesus about those times.

For the most part I feel appreciated.

I do wish that the hard work at home I am appreciated for was seen as hard work. It's difficult to spend time cleaning a room or doing dishes after a long day to only have items left astray later on messing up the work I just completed.

3

But I Need Appreciation!

Let me tell you a story about a man who was minding his own business one day when suddenly, God spoke to him. "I want you to deliver my words to your people," God said (I'm paraphrasing here). "You're going to be my prophet."

"Uh, but God, I'm young. I don't know how to be a prophet," the man answered.

"Don't make excuses," God said. "I'll put my words in your mouth, and you'll say what I tell you to say. Now, listen up . . ." And God proceeded to give the young man the words He wanted him to proclaim.

Sounds good so far, right? God gives you an important job. Makes you His messenger, even. And because you don't know how to do the job, He tells you exactly what to say. Everything's all well and good, maybe even a little exciting, until . . .

"Oh, by the way," God says a few chapters later. "You're going to speak all these words to the people, but they're not going to listen. You'll call to them, but they won't answer you" (see Jer. 1; 7:27).

Wait a minute. What did God say? Did He really say, "Here, go do this important job to which I am calling you, but don't expect to be appreciated for it"?

Yep. He did. And it's similar to what He says to moms today. "I've given you the most important job on earth. Feed my littlest sheep. Build a family. But don't expect to be fully appreciated."

Great. Just great. That's not exactly what we were hoping to hear. We would have much preferred it if God had said, "Feed my littlest sheep. Build a family. You can expect to receive daily expressions of love, gratitude and appreciation from your husband, each of your children and everybody else you know. Maybe even some strangers."

But He didn't. Instead, He called us to serve people who won't fully appreciate us, and that's a dilemma. We have this need inside of us to feel appreciated, yet we're destined not to get it fully met. What do we do? How do we live that way?

In the next chapter, we'll answer those questions. We'll look at what to do about our dilemma—how to get our need met fully and completely. But first, we need to understand more about where this need came from, as well as how we often fail to understand what our need really is and try to fulfill it in inappropriate ways that will never truly satisfy.

Lately I have concluded that what feels like loneliness is often that God-shaped vacuum inside. We, as Christians, get that filled by Jesus, but not perfectly, because we are not perfect and our faith and obedience aren't perfect, so our fellowship with Him cannot be perfect. And sometimes that feels kind of lonely. We think we need other people, and we do; but they can't ultimately fulfill us in all the ways we need. —Karen F.

The Need to Give

Even more basic than our need to feel appreciated is our need to give. I'll admit that I didn't always see it that way. I thought my most basic need was a little (or a lot!) of R&R—the ability to sit down and relax and not have to *do* anything. Preferably, this would take place on a beach somewhere, with crystal-clear water beckoning to me if I felt like getting up off the lounge, and waiters circulating nearby, ready to bring me snacks or some juice with a little umbrella in it.

When I became a mom, especially after I had four little ones in less than five years—and now I have five little ones—this "ultimate need" grew even stronger. If my husband and I could only take a vacation . . . if I could only have a regular spa day . . . if I could just go to the bathroom by myself . . .

The need to unwind, to be completely at rest, was my most important need—or so I thought at the time.

I was wrong.

In reality, our most important need as women, wives, and moms is not to have all opportunities for giving removed; our most important need is to *give*.

Why? Because we're made in God's image, and God is a giver.

Check out this verse in the book of Malachi: "Bring the full tithe into the storehouse, that there may be food in my house. And thereby put me to the test, says the LORD of hosts, if I will not open the windows of heaven for you and pour down for you a blessing until there is no more need" (Mal. 3:10).

Many of us have heard this verse before. We've taken it to mean that God will always provide for our needs, and indeed He will. But there's another, even more basic, meaning in this verse: God is a giver.

And He's a joyful giver. Does this verse sound like God is giving grudgingly? Did He say, "Oh, all right already. Here. The door to the storehouse is open. Take what you need. Just don't waste anything"?

Hardly. Instead, He invites the Israelites to test Him (which, by the way, is the same invitation He offers us today) and says, "If you do, I'll pour out so many blessings upon you that you can't even imagine it."

Now that's the kind of giving I want to receive from God. I'll admit it; I want to have blessings poured out upon me. If you're honest, you'd probably admit that too. Sometimes, as Christians, we get this idea that we're not supposed to want anything from God. We're supposed to be content with whatever He gives us and never desire anything more.

Yes, we're supposed to be content. But that doesn't mean we can't desire to receive from God! True, we dare not attempt to dictate to Him what kind of blessings to give us. He is under no obligation to give us a 4,600-square-foot house, a new Lexus or a month-long vacation to Europe. But He *is* ready and willing to pour out abundant spiritual blessings on us, and it actually makes

God is a joyful giver & we should be too.

Him happy when we ask Him for those blessings. Why? Because He delights in giving.

The only downside, if you can even call it that, of God's being such a generous giver is that He expects us to be that way too. He wants us to give generously and pour out blessings upon those whom He has entrusted to our care, or those with whom we cross paths. And we're to do this not only when those people appreciate us "sufficiently"—after all, God Himself pours out many blessings yet never gets fully appreciated—but all the time.

The apostle Paul refers to God as He who "is able to do immeasurably more than all we ask or imagine" (Eph. 3:20, *NIV*). That's not just because He *can*, but because He wants to. Otherwise, He wouldn't make Himself known to us in such a way. He doesn't say, "I *can* bless you, but I won't." He says, "I can, and I will."

Now, I don't know about you, but I can imagine some pretty wonderful things. Yet this verse tells me that God can do "abundantly more than all [I] ask or imagine." Not just "a little bit" more, but abundantly more. And if the limits of my imagination encompass some pretty amazing things, and God does even a little bit more than that, well . . . WOW! And if He does "abundantly" more than the limits of my imagination, then . . . my mind is blown.

• •

As a parent, I always think, *Am I not giving them enough? Am I giving them too much and spoiling them?* I mean this both materially and emotionally. I want to build them up and support them, but there's a fine line as to how much you can do for them without doing too much and not allowing them to do for themselves. I do know that I have to give generously, and I try to. I want my kids to know that I love them unconditionally, even if I don't give them that new doll or I have to punish them for misbehaving. I know that eventually they'll get it. As an adult and a parent themselves, they'll understand. So I just keep trying and hoping that they realize I'm not perfect but I love them. —Candy J.

• •

Same for you, I'll bet. All those things you can imagine? Well, multiply them by a factor of "abundantly," and that is what God wants to give you. Pretty incredible, huh?

He's a giver, and an extravagant one, at that.

If giving is God's very nature, and if we are made in the image of God (see Gen.1:26), then we too are to be givers. God loves it when He gives, and He loves it when we give. In fact, Scripture tells us that God loves a cheerful giver (see 2 Cor. 9:7).

God doesn't love it nearly as much when my four-year-old asks me to pour her a glass of orange juice, and I sigh before I say, "Okay." That's not cheerful giving.

Well, but what about being tired? Can we really be expected to be cheerful all the time?

Okay, I get that. Believe me, with five young children, I totally get that question. There are days when I'm so tired, worn out or depleted that I can barely muster enthusiasm for a bowl of ice cream, much less for doing yet more work. But even on those days—you've had them too—we are still to be cheerful givers.

Even if I'm tired? Yep. *Even if I've had it up to here?* Yep. *Even if nobody seems to appreciate me?* Yep.

The Need to Be Appreciated

God knows that givers also desire to be appreciated, and He Himself is no exception. When He was about to bring the Israelites into the Promised Land, He told Moses to command them: "And when the LORD your God brings you into the land that he swore to your fathers, to Abraham, to Isaac, and to Jacob, to give you—with great and good cities that you did not build, and houses full of all good things that you did not fill, and cisterns that you did not dig, and vineyards and olive trees that you did not plant—and when you eat and are full, then take care lest you forget the LORD, who brought you out of the land of Egypt, out of the house of slavery" (Deut. 6:10-12).

God wasn't directing the Israelites merely to remember who He was, as they might remember any other fact, such as how to

But I Need Appreciation!   41

turn that manna into food for their families. He wanted them not to forget to be grateful. Not to forget to appreciate Him for what He had done.

So it's natural that we would be like Him in this. We want people to enjoy and appreciate what we do. We want them to be thankful and to "remember" us.

That's why when we go on a vacation, we take pictures. We want to remember the fun times we had. We want to be able to look back at the album (or the digital file on the computer) and say, "Oh yeah, I remember when we did that." But we also want our kids to remember who took them on vacation. We want them to keep in mind that it was Mommy and Daddy who made these experiences possible. The last thing we want is for them to say, "Yeah, I remember that vacation. I wonder who went with me?"

That's what God is talking about when He commands the Israelites to remember Him. He wants them not only to remember their blessings, but to keep in mind that He was responsible for them. It's the same thing He wants from us today.

Going About It the Wrong Way

There's a big difference in the way God wants to be appreciated and the way we do. That difference lies in the fact that we sometimes try to fill our appreciation cup in inappropriate or just plain wrong ways, whereas God never does.

God desires His own glory, and He is completely fulfilled and satisfied when He receives glory from Himself. Not because He's egotistical, but because He knows that He deserves glory. Therefore, He is never without fulfillment.

That's one of the huge differences between God and us. God doesn't depend on receiving glory from humans in order to feel fulfilled, whereas we do. If God receives some glory, we don't mind. But our own glory is what we're really seeking.

Yet other people aren't always going to give us glory. Maybe they don't want to; maybe they can't; maybe they don't know how. God certainly isn't going to give us glory apart from a connection

Megan Breedlove

with Himself. He will never allow us to be satisfied with merely human approval, because He knows that only His approval will truly satisfy us.

Unfortunately, we don't know that, or if we do, we quickly forget. So we seek our own glory. We search for ways to induce other people to tell us how wonderful we are, because we think that will make us feel appreciated and, therefore, fulfilled. The more glory we can get for ourselves, the more fulfilled we are certain that we will feel. Sounds logical, right?

To our human ears, it sounds that way. But it's an idea that is dead wrong.

• •

It's nice to hear from others what a "good job" you are doing, though I find that it's not really necessary. I have had family drama in my life, as others have, and know that NO MATTER WHAT, G-d understands. —Gloria B.

• •

The idea that glory for oneself will be satisfying is exactly what Satan thought back when he was the most beautiful angel in all of God's creation and was named Lucifer. He was certain that seeking his own glory would bring him the satisfaction he desired. So He convinced a third of the angels to follow Him and tried to usurp God's place.

Did Satan's plan bring him the glory he desired? Hardly. Instead, it got him and his followers thrown out of heaven. We read in Isaiah 14:12-15 that Satan got cast into a pit, which we know as hell. And someday, Satan will be consigned to hell for the rest of eternity, no longer able to wreak havoc upon God's children.

Doesn't sound like Satan got what he thought he would or even anything close. He got the complete opposite—as far opposite as it was possible to get.

Fortunately, God will not cast us out of heaven, because Christ's perfect righteousness stands in for ours. My point is that seeking our own glory never brings what we think it will. Instead of bringing us unending satisfaction, it only makes us want more and more in a fruitless effort to be satisfied. It's like drugs, where using them will only increase the amount you have to use next time in order to get the same high. Receiving glory is indeed like getting high in that it makes us feel great! It makes us feel like we're on top of the world! But like a person who uses drugs, we will eventually come down from our glory-induced high, and we'll want more. We'll *need* more in order to feel equally fulfilled. It's a vicious spiral that tears us down even while it pretends to build us up.

Why is this true? Why doesn't receiving glory for ourselves fill our need for appreciation? Doesn't it seem self-evident that when we have people telling us how wonderful we are, we'll feel fulfilled?

It seems that way. But like many things in life, it's deceiving.

The reason why seeking our fulfillment from others doesn't really work is because it violates one of God's cardinal principles: We are to love others. We are to love them so deeply and so well that all men will know that we are Christ's disciples (see John 13:35). Why are the principles of loving others and needing to receive glory from them contradictory? Simply this: if we depend on people to fulfill us, we're not loving them, we're using them.

Using them? But they're *supposed* to meet our needs. After all, our husbands are commanded to lay down their lives for us. Surely a little appreciation isn't too much to ask. And would it be too much to ask for a little gratitude from our children, for whom we do everything? And maybe from friends and family and the society to which we contribute so much? Isn't it legitimate to expect a little appreciation now and then?

Yes . . . and no.

Yes, our husbands should desire to meet our needs (just as we should desire to meet theirs). Yes, our children, depending on their ages, might be expected to express some appreciation for what we do for them. We may legitimately expect these things from those we love, because they should respond appropriately to God's direction in and calling upon their lives. But neither our husband nor our children should ever be expected to fulfill us, because God has not made our fulfillment their job. When we *do* expect them to fulfill us, we're placing a task upon them that God never assigned. We're burdening them with something they were never meant to bear, and we're setting them up for failure and setting ourselves up for disappointment and disillusionment.

If that's the case, are we doomed to feel empty and unappreciated forever? Should we just resign ourselves to doing life on empty, because that's the best it's ever going to get?

No. God's plan is for us to feel *completely* loved, appreciated and fulfilled, not just sometimes, but all the time. If it sounds too good to be true, it's not. It's reality.

How can this happen? There are some things we need to do and some things only God can do. We'll study our part in chapter 4 and God's part in chapter 5.

Going Deeper

Tell God about all the things you can "ask or imagine" that He will do for you in the area of making you feel appreciated. Tell Him you know that His ideas about what to do are even more incredible than yours.

happiness
full life w/ John & cab
calming of body & spirit ab#2

4

So What Do I Do?

The book of Proverbs tells us that hope deferred makes the heart sick (see Prov. 13:12). That's very true in the case of a mom who has felt empty for a long time. The people around her might not express appreciation much, if at all, and even God may not seem to be doing much to help. She tries everything she can think of to make things better for herself—scheduling activities, calling friends, reading self-help books or simply willing herself to feel better. None of it works, and gradually she loses hope that things will ever be any different. Her heart becomes sick.

Gradually, she loses her joy. If she's married, her marriage is perhaps convenient but definitely not vibrant. Parenting isn't much fun anymore, if at all. She doesn't delight in her kids anymore, though she wants to. She may begin to feel guilty and wonder if there is something wrong with her, or whether it's nobody's fault but just the way things are destined to be forever. Her spiritual connection with God is practically nonexistent. She may still read her Bible, but if she does, she doesn't get much out of it. God isn't intimately personal anymore. She feels like she's lost Him too.

We've all been in this position, to some extent, at one time or another. It's not a good place to be. Nobody wants to live this way, but when we're there, we don't see a way out.

Even if you're not at the bottom of the spiral, you will still feel unappreciated at times. How do I know? Because you are a fallen human being, living among fallen human beings. People will say or do things to you, or fail to say and do things, and you will feel unappreciated.

So let's look at four things you can do any time you find yourself feeling empty—whether a little empty or all the way dry. These are simple things to do, things you can put into practice immediately, whenever the emptiness hits, right wherever you are.

Truly Accept That No Other
Human Being Can Fill You Completely

I'm not talking here about a simple intellectual assent to the fact that others will not completely fill your cup. Perhaps you've been reading this book and nodding along with it, thinking, *Yes, that's right.* That's not the level of acceptance I'm talking about.

It's been said that the longest distance in the world is the 18 inches between the head and the heart. It's often fairly easy to accept something with the head—to say, "Yes, I know that's true." But unless that acceptance travels 18 inches downward to the heart, you haven't truly accepted it as fact.

Likewise, it's easy to say, "Oh, I know my husband can't meet all my needs," or "I know my children won't fulfill me." Ditto with friends and family and with society. We've accepted it with the head, but we haven't come to terms with this knowledge in the heart.

We know it's true, but we don't want to believe it. So we continue to nag or manipulate others into fulfilling us. Emotionally, we feel like we can't live on the amount of appreciation we receive, and we're desperate for more. Or perhaps we're resigned to the lack of appreciation and we're deeply sad.

To the degree that you feel you "have" to have more expressed appreciation from others and are desperate to get it from them, you have not accepted the fact that those same people cannot provide you what you need. To the extent that you feel resigned and sad, you have not realized that God has a plan that can leave you completely fulfilled.

The first step in doing everything you can toward seeking greater fulfillment the *right* way is to make peace with the fact that others cannot give you everything you need. Decide that is okay with you. Whether or not those people are actually sinning and truly should be doing better, determine that what they do or don't do isn't going to steal your joy. You are not going to make your contentment dependent on other people's actions. You can be deeply contented even while you wish for better. Trust me on this one. After awhile, you won't even be wishing as much that other people would do better, because you will be finding your contentment elsewhere, from a Source that will never fail.

• •

The journey of motherhood is not without its bumps in the road. When my husband and I moved to Texas from Illinois a month after our daughter was born, it was a homecoming for him. For me, it uprooted me from my family and friends, and the church that I had been a part of for 15 years. My support system was yanked out from underneath me. It was extremely emotional for me. I learned more than ever to rely upon God and the gifts and talents He placed in me. God has given you the precious children in your life for a reason. Go to God, cry out to Him, ask for His strength and guidance. He will answer you, maybe not the way that you expect or want, but He does love you and will help you. —Carol W.

• •

Stop Panicking When Your Needs Aren't Met

I have to admit that this one applies to me as much as to anybody else out there.

Case in point: The other day, my husband took our children out with him to run errands so that I could get the house clean. (This was actually a treat for me, not some kind of punishment.) I worked hard for a couple of hours, and when Phil came home, the house looked great. I just knew Phil would shower me with compliments about all that I'd managed to accomplish.

Only . . . he didn't. Because he had given me as much time as he could to get my cleaning done, he only had a minute or two before he had to turn around and leave for work. So he breezed into the house, headed straight for our bedroom at the back of the house and began changing into his dress clothes.

I gave him a minute or so to realize he "should have" complimented me right off. Didn't happen. So I went and stood in the doorway. "So . . ." I said in that hint-hint voice, "how's the house look?"

"Oh, it looks great," he said. "I was going to tell you that." And he went back to tying his shoes.

I'll admit it: I stood there and thought, *That's it? That's all the compliments I get for all I did?*

So I said, "You really think so?"

Now, here's the point: Why did I ask that second question? After he told me the house looked great, why did I ask, "Do you really think so?"

You know the answer, because you've done it too. It was because he hadn't filled my appreciation cup "sufficiently" with his first compliment. And *I needed more.*

That's what I'm talking about—that feeling right there that says "the amount of appreciation I received was not enough, and I must have more."

Had I been willing to feel a little empty for a fraction of a second, I could have dealt with the situation properly. I could have thought it over and realized that my husband is a truthful man, and he gave me a great compliment, so he really didn't need to say any more. But I wasn't willing. I wanted more appreciation, I wanted it now, and I wanted him to give it to me.

That's generally what happens when we aren't willing to feel empty for even a short time. The feeling of emptiness arises, and we panic. We *must* have appreciation, and we must have it *right now*! So what do we do? We begin to manipulate people in order to get them to give us what we want. We (although perhaps politely) demand it from them, and we get irritated if they don't give it.

My second question to my husband was manipulative. I wasn't really asking whether he meant what he had said. I knew that he did. My husband never lies. I was actually telling him that I needed more affirmation, and I disguised my demand as a question because I didn't want to look peevish or needy by asking straight out. I chose to manipulate instead of being straightforward.

Do you ever try to manipulate others into giving you the affirmation you want? If you don't think so, consider whether you ever find yourself having the following conversations.

Someone tells you that you look great today, and you say, "Oh, really?" not because you don't believe them, but because you secretly want to hear them say it again.

A coworker compliments you on a project, and you thank the person, but then you tell her about all the difficult obstacles you overcame in order to complete the project so that she can fully appreciate you and tell you so.

It's possible to have these conversations without being manipulative. It's all in the intent. If you are trying to get something from somebody that you aren't asking for directly, that's manipulation. It's using people. It's treating them as objects to satisfy our own needs rather than focusing on loving them and meeting their needs.

. . . .

We all want our families to acknowledge our hard work. But I think we can get stuck in the trap of only working for the approval of other people. I'm slowly learning to see the things I do for my husband and children as being a steward of the blessings God has given me. In that case, I really should be seeking God's approval alone. —Carla L.

. . . .

That's why we need to be comfortable enough with feeling empty, at least briefly, that we won't begin to treat people this way. We need to remain calm instead of panicking. Feeling empty won't kill us for a long time, much less for a short time.

That's what we'll talk about in the next section.

Emptiness Is Not a Death Sentence

Did you read that subhead and respond, "Yeah, but it feels like it"? Several years ago, I would have responded that way too. But I'm here to tell you that emptiness will not kill you. Not if you see it as an opportunity instead of a curse.

An opportunity? You've got to be kidding.

· ·

Every time I don't deal with my anger, I allow the root of bitterness to grow in my heart. The other day, my husband was speaking unkindly to me, at least in my opinion. I did not lose my
temper, but calmly tried to tell him that he'd hurt my feelings. He
refused to agree with me and apologize. I realized then that I had
a choice: I could either stay angry and let bitterness grow, or I
could go to the Lord and ask Him to take my anger from me and
help me to forgive. I did the latter and felt such peace. The next
day, my husband did apologize, and I forgave him. Yet even without his apology, the Lord had given me peace. —Mary L.

· ·

Nope. I'm not kidding. This was one of the lessons God taught
me in dealing with having my appreciation cup filled, and though
it was a hard lesson for me, it was also one of the most valuable
lessons I've learned. Emptiness will not kill me. It doesn't even
have to hurt me very much. The idea that a lack of appreciation
must do me harm is a lie, and guess where all lies ultimately have
their roots?

All lies originate with Satan. He "was a murderer from the beginning, and does not stand in the truth, because there is no truth
in him. When he lies, he speaks out of his own character, for he is
a liar and the father of lies" (John 8:44). I'm sure he loves it when
believing his lies causes us to turn against each other—especially
against our husbands, with whom we are one flesh, or against our
brothers and sisters in Christ, with whom we are co-members of
one body, that is, Christ's.

So if you feel empty for a minute—if someone has failed to appreciate you the way you wanted him or her to—realize this is not
going to kill you emotionally. You can stand it. It's a lie that you
have to go under because of what that other person failed to say.

Not only is emptiness *not* a death sentence, but it *is* also an opportunity. *Opportunity for what*? you ask, with good reason. Many
of us have had a difficult childhood, or even a difficult adulthood,
and we've had plenty of opportunity to feel hurt and grieved. Who
needs any more opportunities like that?

But that's not what I'm talking about. I'm talking about an opportunity to spend a little time with God that you might not have spent otherwise.

• •

Rebekah S. tells of one evening when she had an argument with her husband and got pretty angry. "I walked outside with the dog and looked at the stars," she says, "and all I could pray was 'Change my heart, O God!' because I knew I hadn't responded properly."

• •

If you're like me, you have good intentions about reading your Bible, praying and spending uninterrupted time with the Lord. But if you're like me in another way, you often get distracted by the myriad other tasks awaiting you, and you forget Him. Have you ever found yourself getting into bed at night and thinking, *Oops! Forgot to have my quiet time today.* Yeah, me too. And if that's the case, feeling empty is a great reminder to spend time with God.

When someone shows you less appreciation than what you hoped for, instead of manipulating him or her, or feeling angry or depressed, you have another option. You could pray. Why not take a minute right then, just after the words have been said (or should have been said), to connect with your heavenly Father? Instead of saying, "Do you *really*, honey?" you could say silently, "God, thank You for a husband who appreciates me. More than that, thank You that *You* appreciate me. Thank You that You see this thing that I did, and You appreciate it."

• •

One of the biggest weaknesses in my life has been seeking others' approval. I suppose this stemmed from not having much self-esteem growing up and never quite belonging to the "in crowd." I would tailor my words and actions to mimic those of people around me that I viewed as "having it all together" or "popular" or even "godly," which sounds far more impressive. As a young

wife, and then as a young mother, I remember trying be
like one of the pastors' wives in our church who was
respected and loved by all (I'll call her Nicole). She embodied the
"gentle and quiet spirit" we read about in 1 Peter 3:4, and
exemplified a good, loving wife and patient, loving mother. I
tried so hard to be like Nicole, because it was obvious that God
loved and approved of her. At the time, I couldn't fathom that
He loved and approved of me in the same way; therefore, trying
to emulate her seemed like the right thing to do.

Over the next several years, I found myself entirely frustrated
that I wasn't achieving the peace and assurance of God's
approval, and I slowly began to learn that pretending to be
someone else was almost an insult to God and His creativity.
Namely, He created me as unique, unlike anyone else. For me
to impersonate someone else, I was essentially telling Him that
He did a lousy job creating me as me, and I was disposing
of this gift by impersonating someone else.

Professional counseling helped me on this journey, and for
the first time in my life, at the age of 35, I began to LIKE what
God created and who He made me to be. From that point, I was
able to apply faith to His Word and BELIEVE that He was
delighted in me, and that He delighted in saving me from hell
through the gift of His Son, Jesus. Then I began to trust that my
personality could bring glory to God, as I continued to walk in
faith. This also helped in my parenting, in that I was able to
fully enjoy my children for the individuals they were, and I didn't
have to parent like Nicole parented. God wanted ME to
parent MY kids for a reason! —Cindi M.

• •

We'll talk more—a lot more—about how God notices the things
you do and how He feels about them. It's a vitally important point,
and we don't want to miss it. But for now, let's leave that topic and
consider the fourth thing you can do instead of letting a lack of appreciation steal your joy.

Begin Looking to God for Fulfillment

It's not enough merely to stop requiring other people to fill you up. That's a great start, to be sure, but it's insufficient. Tearing yourself away from the primary source (people) where you have been getting your affirmation without replacing it with anything else won't fill the void either. In order to feel truly fulfilled, you not only have to release others from the false obligations to which you have been holding them, but you also have to turn to God and both ask Him and allow Him to fulfill you.

We'll talk more in the next chapter about how God will fill you. First, let's look at your part in all this. Some things only God can do; some things, if you are to reach a place in life where you are truly fulfilled, you must do.

Put Yourself in a Position to Hear from God

This might sound obvious, but it usually doesn't work out that way in practice: We need to place ourselves in a position to hear from God. Granted, God absolutely can and does speak whenever and wherever He wants, to whomever He wants. There's no doubt about that. But there's also no doubt that He speaks more to those who show that they want to hear from Him.

In fact, God's Word promises, "And it shall come to pass, that before they call, I will answer; and while they are yet speaking, I will hear" (Isa. 65:24, *KJV*). Originally, this passage was referring to the Israelites. But it also applies to us today. Allow me to paraphrase: "Before [a mom] calls, I will answer; and while [she is] yet speaking, I will hear."

Pretty awesome, isn't it? God is so eager to talk to us that even before we call on Him, He already has an answer in mind, and He is moved to care even before we finish speaking. If your heart is right toward God, He is waiting and eager to talk to you, to answer you and to show you that He cares about you. Right now, as you sit reading this book, He cares. Later, as you go to bed, He cares. Tomorrow morning, as you get up for another day of the same ol' same ol', He cares.

God doesn't always wait until we approach Him before He speaks to us. Nonetheless, we need to make the effort to keep up our end of the relationship. It's disrespectful to take God for granted and just fly through the day, not really paying Him much attention, yet expecting Him to speak regularly to us.

• •

My personal time with God is one of the most important things I need, but it's one of the most difficult things to find. If left to my once daily thinking of "When the kids get to bed, or as soon as I'm done with this . . . or that," it never happens. Not for me. So my time with God, where I focus on talking to Him and listening, is done on my way to work in the morning. I cover the day for myself, my family and any other requests, and just be with Him for the drive (about 30 minutes or so). At lunch and on any downtime during the day at my desk, I will read my Bible. My time is in spurts. Good or bad, those "spurts" sustain me. I have time at night once everyone is in bed, as well, but by then I'm exhausted, so it lacks. But scheduling that time like I would a date or appointment works best for me. If I wait until I have time, I will keep Him waiting. —Ashley R.

• •

Don't get me wrong; I'm not saying you have to have a solid hour together each day in order to show Him you're interested. (Remember, I have five kids; I know this is practically impossible.) It's absolutely true that God can and does speak to us through the very ordinary circumstances of our day, and that if we move through our days with a listening, teachable spirit, He understands that we don't have tons of time to sit down by ourselves with Him. But even the busiest mom has five minutes a day to spend with God, with only rare exceptions. When I haven't spent time with God on a particular day, 99.9 percent of the time it's because I haven't bothered to make time. I could carve out five minutes a day if I really wanted to, and so could you.

This is not just legalism. We're not just trying to check off one more thing on our to-do list or earn another star on our Sunday

School chart. Instead, we're showing the Person we love that we're interested in what He has to say. And perhaps even more than that, we're reminding ourselves that we *need* to be interested in talking to Him and hearing from Him.

By doing these four things, we'll make great strides toward ceasing to seek our fulfillment from wrong sources and beginning to seek it from the one true Source. But our own efforts aren't enough. The apostle Paul reminds us that "neither he who plants nor he who waters is anything, but only God, who makes things grow" (1 Cor. 3:7, *NIV*). This applies toward our efforts to gain fulfillment, as well. We can do our part, but in order for it to truly work, God must do His.

Fortunately, He's ready and willing to do just that, as we'll see in the next chapter.

Going Deeper

Is it hard for you to do the four "your part" things mentioned in this chapter? Tell God how hard it is. Ask Him to help you.

_____

_____

_____

_____

_____

_____

_____

_____

_____

_____

_____

5

God's Part

I love it when kids ask questions about God, especially when they're young. They ask some really interesting questions then.

"Mommy, does God know everything?" Lindsey asked once.

"Yes, sweetheart, He knows everything," I answered.

"Like even when I go to the bathroom?" she asked.

"Uh, yeah," I said.

"Eeewww," she replied.

Then there was the time when I was helping three-year-old Ellie get settled in her car seat. I clicked the metal prongs into the buckle-thingy and fastened the latch across her chest. We were good to go, or so I thought. Apparently, Ellie had a question first.

"Mommy, is God everywhere?" she asked.

"Yes, He is," I said.

"Even when we go somewhere in the car?"

"Even then."

She extended her arm and pointed to the floorboards with her forefinger. "Is He *right down there*?"

Yes, God is everywhere, and yes, He knows everything. Little children wonder at this fact, because they're well aware that their own understanding is limited. They also know they can't be in two places at once.

God and Jesus are always in our daily talk. When my daughter and I are driving around, she will ask the most off-the-wall questions or just life questions, and I know that Jesus is poking Ashley in the arm, saying, "Hey, ask your mom this and see what she says." I feel that God is testing me all the time, and I do love it and do my best with answering her. —Jenny U.

We should be amazed at God too. He's everywhere, and we can only be one place at a time; He knows everything there is to know about everything in the world, and sometimes I don't even know what to fix for supper. His understanding and abilities far, far exceed my own. Any skill or capability I have is only a dim reflection of what He can do.

Not only is God incredibly *able*, but He has also made all His power and abilities available on my behalf and yours. Think of it—the same power that created the universe is available to *us*. The same hands that formed all of creation are available to form the very circumstances of our lives. The same knowledge that knows things like where the wind comes from and how to make mountains (see the book of Job, chapters 38–41, for all kinds of incredible things God knows) is available to help *us* with our problems.

. . . .

I went into labor early one morning and we rushed to the hospital. All was going well; then it came time to push. The nurses told me a first-time mom could push up to two hours. The first time I saw her she was gray and was rushed to the NICU team. Her APGAR score was 1. I was in shock. Exhausted from pushing, excited that I would finally get to meet my daughter, yet worried that something was wrong. The NICU staff was able to get her breathing. I learned later that she got stuck in the birth canal and was so traumatized from being stuck and the pushing. It was what they call a depressed birth. Her little body just shut down. A little more than 24 hours later, I was able to hold my daughter. I will never forget that moment. She had already been such a fighter. I looked down and said, "Hi, baby girl." She looked up at me with instant recognition and, as funny as it may sound, she had a look of relief as if she was saying "Ahhh . . . this is my mommy!" This child is a gift for as long or short a time as God allows me to be her mom. Giving my child fully to God isn't a one-time thing. It's often a daily thing. And it's hard. I love her so much, and it's hard to fathom that someone loves her way beyond my abilities. —Michelle M.

. . . .

Most of us don't really think about how much God can help us with our day-to-day lives. Sure, we pray prayers like, "Please, God, let my baby sleep through the night" (I've prayed that one a lot lately) or "God, don't let my husband lose his job." Both of those are good and valid prayers. We're supposed to bring our requests to God. In fact, we're commanded to do so (see Phil. 4:6). The problem is not that we make requests of God. The problem is that our requests are too small, in that we only seek God's responses to our requests and fail to seek God Himself.

Usually that's because we don't understand the benefits of seeking God Himself. We can easily see the benefits of a fat bank account, a new car or a housekeeper and are easily motivated to pray for these things. But God Himself? We regard this as a rather vague, ethereal, spiritual benefit that doesn't have a lot of practicality in the world we have to live in. How will a relationship with God help us in the day to day? We don't get it. So we spend all of our time pleading with Him for His benefits without asking for the greatest Benefit of all.

C. S. Lewis wrote, in *The Weight of Glory*, "Our Lord finds our desires, not too strong, but too weak. We are half-hearted creatures, fooling about with drink and sex and ambition when infinite joy is offered us, like an ignorant child who wants to go on making mud pies in a slum because he cannot imagine what is meant by the offer of a holiday at the sea. We are far too easily pleased."[1]

We need to do more than seek a divine strategy for getting people to do the things we think they ought to do. We need to seek the divine Himself.

But how will a relationship with God help us feel fulfilled? Wouldn't there be more payoff in getting other people to compliment us than in spending a few minutes in prayer?

No, no, no. A thousand times, no. It's a lie straight from Satan that *anything* could be of more help to us than our relationship with God. We are deceived into believing—or simply fail to understand—the benefits of intimacy with God, which, in Satan's eyes, is just as good.

• •

Ever since I was little, my desire was to have 6 to 8 children,
about 15 to 18 months apart. Well, when my husband
and I got married, we had decided we wanted to wait five years
to start having children. I was fine with that. A few months
into our marriage, I got pregnant. We were happy; the dream of
starting a family happened a little quicker than planned,
but we were thrilled nonetheless. Shortly after my son was
born, I was ready to try for number two. My plan, again,
was not to be God's plan. When my son was six months old, I
had the first of six miscarriages in about a two-and-a-half-year
period. I was starting to get really angry inside, and frustrated.
Then, following those years of miscarriage, there were a few
years of infertility. I was bitter and angry at God. I was so
focused on what I didn't have that I couldn't be thankful for
what I did have. Finally, one night after a family Christmas party,
I wrestled with God, so to speak. That Christmas, at my
grandma's, there were two new additions to the family,
my nephew and a cousin's baby. I was so angry at God that I
couldn't enjoy the day. I had to leave early. That week my husband was out of town and I sent my son to my mother-in-law's
for the day. I spent the day in the Word, crying out to God, praying. I felt so much better and finally had some peace in my heart.
God finally showed me He was in charge of my life, not me, and I
needed to trust in Him. —Dana C.

• •

Precious mom, God *is* life. He's not something you *add to* your
life; He *is* your life. Jesus said, "I am the way, the truth, and the life"
(John 14:6, *KJV*). Apart from Him, you don't have life. I'm not even
talking at the moment about those who have no relationship with
Him at all and are destined for eternal death. I'm talking about
those who are truly Christians but don't understand that apart
from Jesus, there is no vibrancy. No joy. No living life to the fullest,
because apart from Him, there is no life.

Any shred of joy or delight that we experience in this lifetime
is because of Him. Any appreciation we receive (if it is good and

righteous) ultimately comes through Him. Any fulfillment we experience is because of Him and cannot be separated from Him.

· ·

The greatest gift you can give your children is your unconditional love. It has the ability to cover a myriad of mothering sins and helps them have perseverance as they grow. Having unconditional love from their parents also makes them more open and accepting of God's unconditional love for them. —Gina M.

· ·

How does this work? How does Christ turn a humdrum daily existence into life abundant (see John 10:10)?

He does it in amazing, revolutionary, truth-filled ways that are available to every mom, regardless of whether she's single or married, whether she has 1 child or 10, whether her house looks like Martha Stewart lives there (there has to be *somebody* out there like that, right?), or she's standing in the middle of a kitchen floor covered in Cheerios and dog hair.

His ways of giving us abundant, fulfilling life are exactly what we're going to look at in this chapter.

God Makes Himself Available to You

We've already touched on this, but this truth is so incredible that it bears further exploration. Think about it—the God of the vast, unreachable universe cares about the tiny speck named (insert your name here). The psalmist marveled at this too, writing, "What is man that you are mindful of him, and the son of man that you care for him?" (Ps. 8:4).

Have you ever stopped to think how amazing it is that God has made Himself available to you?

Look at it this way: if you want to see the President of the United States, you have to do more than just march into the Oval Office, plop yourself down in an armchair and start talking. You wouldn't get anywhere even near the inside of the White House without going through proper security, much less into the inner sanctum of the President's office. You can't get physically close to the President without being thoroughly screened by multiple layers of security designed to ensure that no unauthorized person gets close to him.

Even if you have a squeaky-clean criminal background check, and you're dressed appropriately (yes, there is a dress code), that still doesn't guarantee you an audience with the President. You have to somehow get put on his appointment schedule. That means that other people will decide who the President would most benefit from seeing, and that's who gets on his schedule. If you don't have important politics to discuss with him, or you're not a veteran or haven't rescued a small child in a highly public incident, you don't have a chance. Just being a member of his constituency isn't enough. You have to have a reason to see him that's better than all the other reasons of all the other people wanting to see him. Even then, you only get 15 minutes, and then you're outta there. You don't get the chance to overstay your welcome. If you try, you will be escorted out.

Yet God, who is far greater than any person who will ever sit behind the desk of the Oval Office, is always available to you. A criminal background won't keep you from Him; He welcomes anybody. Being dressed "wrong" won't keep you from Him; He'll listen to you no matter how you're dressed. Having an insufficient reason won't keep you from Him; there's no such thing as an insufficient reason.

You won't be limited to 15 minutes (though 15 minutes is more than most of us usually spend with Him on a daily basis). You can have as long as you want, anytime you want. God keeps office hours 24/7/365, and He even puts in an extra day on Leap Year. He doesn't sandwich you in between other more pressing duties; there is no more pressing engagement for Him than meeting with you. If your appointment with God gets missed, it's not because He didn't show up; it's because you didn't.

In order to see the President, you have to be somebody important. But as far as God is concerned, you already are somebody important. Therefore, He has made Himself available to you any-time you want Him. The problem is that most of us don't want Him very often.

"I will be found by you, declares the LORD" (Jer. 29:14). But most of us don't seek Him very often unless we need something. Rarely do we seek Him for His sake alone.

Knowing this truth should fill you with a sense of incredible significance. God says you're important enough to be available for you at any time. You can come before His throne any time you like and be welcomed, because you're *that* important. With or without an appointment.

· ·

I grew up in a fairly dysfunctional family. These days, it might be called abusive. Dad was an alcoholic, and Mom was very code-pendent. Brother had a chronic illness, so someone had to be there to be a stress relief. That was my job in the family. I wanted my children to know the love that I never felt from my family. I had grown up with people who said "I love you" but who often created conditions. During my teen years, my mother often told me "I love you, but I don't like you." As my second son exerted his strong personality, I was torn. I resisted harsh discipline but feared that a lack of discipline might mean that I was creating more problems for him. Most disturbing of all was the anger that I started feeling toward him. I felt the anger from my own child-hood family experiences combined with the anger that he would be escaping the situations that I endured despite his inappropri-ate behavior. I prayed and began to reflect that this might be how God feels. We keep failing at the most simple tasks: loving our neighbor, forgiving and staying faithful to His Word. I taught my children the phrase "I love you, no matter what." Sometimes I would quiz them—"What could you do that would stop me from loving you?" My son often created elaborate, creative situations. I always told him, "That would make me sad or angry, but I would still love you." It was hard to understand God as a loving father—I saw Him more as a stern, disapproving father (like my own). But when I started to see God through the eyes of a parent, I began to understand how God could love us despite the trials and tribulations we create. I began to think that maybe I was good enough for His love. —Kate E.

• •

God loves You

Jesus loves me, this I know, for the Bible tells me so.

Millions, maybe even billions, of people know that song. You're probably one of them. But how many of those people see it as more than just a children's Sunday School song? How many see it as a statement of incredible truth *and are moved by it?*

Not many. That's because either we take God's love for granted and therefore become blasé about it, or we don't really think He means it the way we'd like Him to.

Yeah, yeah, Jesus loves me. I know that.

I hope this truth is alive and well and making a life-changing difference in your heart. If not, why did it stop being something that amazes you and become something that fails to impress you because you've heard it before? Could it be that you don't really understand what His love entails?

God doesn't love you in the same way you might love corn dogs (or, as a dear friend of mine pronounces it, "cawhrn dawgs"). Some days, you're all about corn dogs; other days, you could take them or leave them. Fortunately, God's love is much more consistent. He loves you all the time, not just on the days when you're fun to be around, when your heart is right or when you make it a priority to meet with Him for some prayer time, but every day. He loves you constantly and consistently. His level of love does not change depending on what you do or don't do; it always stays the same, because it proceeds from His loving character and is dependent on *His* nature, not on yours.

Even when you make mistakes, He loves you. Even when you sin willfully, He loves you. Even when you have no clue about spiritual things and spend most of the day not even thinking about

Him, He loves you. He doesn't sort-of love you on some days and really love you on others. He loves you big-time, all the time.

. . . .

"I almost had an affair, and God still loves me," JoAnna M. says. "I almost did what I said I'd never do. Yet He has forgiven me and still loves me."

. . . .

In fact, Zephaniah 3:17 tells us that "The LORD your God is in your midst, a mighty one who will save; he will rejoice over you with gladness; he will quiet you by his love; he will exult over you with loud singing."

Rejoice? Exult? *Loud singing?*

That doesn't sound to me like a God who just sort-of loves me. And He doesn't just sort-of love you either. It's not a "for God so loved the world, and I'm in the world, therefore He's obligated to love me too" kind of love (I used to believe that). It's a madly passionate, joyful love that rejoices in the presence of His beloved—you!

Yes, *you.*

It doesn't matter what you've done; it doesn't matter how you've failed in the past or are in the midst of failing right now. God has chosen to love you. Not because of your merit or lack thereof, but because He loves you. His love is not dependent on you; it's dependent on Him.

It doesn't matter that your parents have convinced you that you aren't very lovable, or that society has done that, or that you've never thought of yourself as anything special. God says you're wrong. He says you *are* special. He says you're worth exulting over.

Dictionary.com gives two definitions for "exult": 1. to show or feel a lively or triumphant joy; rejoice exceedingly; be highly elated or jubilant; and 2. to leap, especially for joy. My friend, *that* is how God feels about you. It's not just an obligatory love, but a wildly passionate love for you. His emotions go crazy when He thinks of you.

Recently, my four older children went to stay with my husband's parents for a week of VBS. Jessica, four years old, had mixed feelings. She dearly loves her grandparents, but she wasn't sure if she would have a good time being so far away from home. So I spent some time helping her think of things she and Grandma would get to do together.

Remembering one of her favorite activities, I said, "Hey, I have an idea!"

I definitely had her attention. "How about you and Grandma could make cookies?" I suggested.

Jessica's eyes widened, and her mouth dropped open in a huge, amazed grin.

My friend, *that's* the reaction God has when He thinks of spending time with you. He doesn't just shrug His shoulders and say, "Okay, whatever." He rejoices *exceedingly*. He delights. He sings out His joy in loud melody.

This kind of extravagant love is what we long for. This kind of love is what will fulfill us. We think that receiving mere verbal expressions from ordinary human beings will fill our appreciation cup. Nope. Okay, maybe they put a few drops in the cup. But it's God's love that will make our cup runneth over.

To which source of love and appreciation are you looking? Do you feel loved, appreciated and fulfilled? If you don't, you know where to look. Don't wait any longer. Don't try to live on the dregs of what imperfect human beings offer you. Run to the true Source, the Fountain of Life, from whom is every good and perfect gift (see James 1:17). You'll find love and appreciation beyond your wildest dreams, and who doesn't want that?

Going Deeper

Isn't it amazing what God will do for you and how He feels about you? Tell Him how amazing His love is and ask Him to do for you what He's promised He will do.

6

Loving Jesus

There was a time earlier on in my mothering when I felt pretty sorry for myself.

I had two children then. Ellie was about two, and Kenny would have been about six months. As you know, there is a lot of work involved in raising two little people, especially as young as my little people were at the time. And I was getting burnt out on it.

I knew that being a mom mattered, that building character into my children's lives mattered—the big things. But what about the little things? What about all the diapers, the jars of baby food and the endless loads of laundry? Toys all over the place, diaper bags to pack any time I went somewhere, car seats to adjust and sticky hands and faces to wipe clean? Not to mention bath time, bedtime and *more* diapers. Do *these* things matter?

To make matters worse, I told myself that anybody could do what I was doing. After all, making a PBJ sandwich doesn't take any particular skill. Neither does changing the bag in the diaper pail or running a bathtub full of water. *Is this what my life has come down to?* I wondered. Tasks that anybody could do, that nobody notices or cares about? Unless, of course, I *don't* do them?

Maybe you can identify with me. Maybe you've had these thoughts, as well as the resultant feelings of discouragement and frustration. If so, you know it's not fun to feel that what you do doesn't really make a big difference, that all the time and effort you put into your mothering is like throwing money down a hole— you do it, and then *pfft!* it's gone, with not much to show for it.

You can tell that I was not in a good place, emotionally or spiritually, at least in terms of this issue. I had begun to deal with the issue of God's love for me and accept that He really did love me. But I had no idea how much He also appreciated me.

Until, that is, God got tired of listening to me whine and complain, and He broke into my pity party. *You're wrong that what you do doesn't matter*, He said. *Remember what My Son said about "that which you do for the least of these?"*

· ·

I once heard Oprah say that when a child walks into a room, he or she should see a light go on in his or her parents' eyes. And that always stuck with me. How if children don't receive validation of their worth from their parents, how will they ever believe that they are truly worthy as human beings? —Megan D.

· ·

In my desire to know more, I looked in my concordance for some clue as to where the longer passage was located. I found it in Matthew 25:

"When the Son of Man comes in his glory, and all the angels with him, then he will sit on his glorious throne. Before him will be gathered all the nations, and he will separate people one from another as a shepherd separates the sheep from the goats. And he will place the sheep on his right, but the goats on the left. Then the King will say to those on his right, 'Come, you who are blessed by my Father, inherit the kingdom prepared for you from the foundation of the world. For I was hungry and you gave me food, I was thirsty and you gave me drink, I was a stranger and you welcomed me, I was naked and you clothed me, I was sick and you visited me, I was in prison and you came to me.' Then the righteous will answer him, saying, 'Lord, when did we see you hungry and feed you, or thirsty and give you drink? And when did we see you a stranger and welcome you, or naked and clothe you? And when did we see you sick or in prison and visit you?' And the King will answer them, 'Truly, I say to you, as you did it to one of the least of these my brothers, you did it to me.'

"Then he will say to those on his left, 'Depart from me, you cursed, into the eternal fire prepared for the devil and his angels. For I was hungry and you gave me no food, I was thirsty and you gave me no drink, I was a stranger and you did not welcome me, naked and you did not clothe me, sick and in prison and you did not visit me.' Then they also will answer, saying, 'Lord, when did we see you hungry or thirsty or a stranger or naked or sick or in prison, and did not minister to you?' Then he will answer them, saying, 'Truly, I say to you, as you did not do it to one of the least of these, you did not do it to me.' And these will go away into eternal punishment, but the righteous into eternal life" (Matt. 25:31-46).

All of a sudden, I realized what God was trying to tell me.

My children were "the least of these"—not because they are worthless, but because children are the least able to help themselves and the least able to adequately repay what you do for them. And Jesus said that whatever I do for the least of these, I do for Him.

He didn't say, "Whatever you do for the least of these, I appreciate it." Nor did He say, "Whatever you do for the least of these, you earn a gold star on your heavenly chart." No, He said that whatever I do for the least of these, it's the exact same thing as doing it directly for Him.

Wow! So if that's true (and because Jesus said it and it's recorded in the Bible, we know that it *is* true), then what I do has incredible significance!

Everything I do for my children, even the little, mundane "nothing" tasks I do as a mom, I do for Jesus! And if *that's* true ... well, then today I fed Him. I clothed Him. I took care of Him. Not, "I took care of my kids on His behalf," but, "I took care of *Him*."

I wrote a poem at the time to try to capture the beautiful truth God had shown me. Although I'm a writer, I'm not usually a poet, but I simply wanted to get down on paper what I had learned. I never realized that anyone beyond my husband and perhaps my small group at church would ever hear the poem, much less love it. But God sent it out all over the world, making something of it far beyond what I expected. I think its truth will resonate with you as well.

Loving Jesus
I started my day early,
Before the room was light.
I lifted my son from his crib
And wished it was still night.
But as I held him close and said,
"Hi, Kenneth, precious one,"
I knew that as I greeted him,
I greeted too God's Son.

When my daughter woke up later,
Calling, "Mommy! Mommy! Down!"
I picked her up and hugged her
In her worn Elmo nightgown.
I know she felt the closeness
That a mother's touch affords.
I welcomed not just Ellie,
But so, too, the Lord of lords.

That day, I mixed some formula
And opened jars of peas.
I fixed some "pizza butter" bread
When she grinned and said, "Pleeeeease."
I heated up some leftovers;
I had to nuke them twice.
And when I fed my children,
I was feeding Jesus Christ.

I made some funny faces,
And "played puzzles" on the floor.
I dressed kitties, ran around outside,
And played with them some more.

Megan Breedlove

We laughed and jumped and tickled,
Making memories to be stored.
When I spent time with my children,
I spent time with my Lord.

I wiped up sticky cereal
And washed the dishes clean.
I straightened, picked up, put away,
And dusted in between.
I did six loads of laundry
And folded it like new.
When I cleaned for my children,
I cleaned for my Savior, too.

When my children were both crying,
I held them in my arms.
I cuddled them and whispered
That I'd keep them safe from harm.
I told them how their Father saved them
With His perfect Lamb.
When I comforted my children,
I comforted I AM.

Later on that evening,
I put them in the bath.
I washed their little bodies
As they kicked around and splashed.
I dried them in soft towels
And put their jammies on.
When I had washed my children's feet,
I'd washed the Holy One.

I cooked and cleaned and rearranged,
Made beds and taught and played.
I made sure that we had food to eat
And that we often prayed.

Megan Breedlove

I died to self. I made a home
From ordinary things.
But when I served my children,
I served the King of kings.

To some, I have done nothing,
But to two, I've done the world.
I made eternal difference
To my precious boy and girl,
And to the One who watches over
Every pathway that I've trod.
For when I've loved my precious children,
I've loved Almighty God.

Precious mom, this is for you. God wants you to know that when you cared for your children today, you cared for His Son. You didn't just do nice, Christian things on God's behalf; you did them to and for Christ Himself.

What you do *matters*.

I want you to imagine something with me for a minute. Let's say you take your precious child to the playground. It's a rare moment: the weather is perfect, everybody's healthy and nothing else is on the schedule. You allow your child to run ahead to the slide as you sit down on a bench where you can easily watch. Holding to the handrails, he carefully climbs to the top, sits down and *whooshes* down the slide.

But when he gets to the bottom, he's going a little too fast, and his little legs can't quite stop the force of his slide. His feet hit the mulch cushioning the ground and he stumbles forward and falls on his face. When he lifts his head from the ground, you see a chunk of mulch fall from his lips as he begins to wail.

Okay. Now let's say there is another little child playing on the merry-go-round nearby. This child turned to watch your son go down the slide. When she sees him fall, she runs over to him. She crouches down in the dirt next to him, brushes the dirt from his face and helps him stand up. "I'm sorry you fell down," you hear her say, and she wraps your son in a sweet and comforting hug.

How would you feel about that little girl? You'd love her too, wouldn't you? Would you be grateful to her for what she did on behalf of your son? Ohhh, yeah!

Here's the point: the woman sitting on the bench represents God the Father; the little boy who fell represents Jesus; and the little girl is you.

That's exactly what Jesus said: you are ministering to Him, not just to your children, but to Him. And when you do, God sees you. He sees you brush Him off, put your arms around Him and love on Him. He knows what you've done for His Son. And if you, a mere human being, would appreciate it when another child helps yours, how do you think God feels when you minister to Jesus?

Yep. Multiply your feelings by a factor of "infinitely," and you begin to come close.

What difference would it make in how you feel about your mothering duties if you realized you are ministering to Christ Himself and that God responds to your efforts with gratitude? I bet you'd feel a whole lot more appreciated than you do now.

Even if no one else on earth expresses it, God appreciates you, and He does express it. How do I know? If you were the mom on the park bench, you wouldn't have ignored the little girl who brushed away your son's tears. You would have gone over there, made sure your son was okay and then thanked the little girl, maybe even with tears in your eyes.

Remember that the next time you think nobody appreciates you, because Someone does.

Going Deeper

How does it make you feel to realize that when you serve your children, you are directly and personally serving Jesus? Talk to Him. Thank Him for receiving your service personally. Offer Him your service to your family as a gift to Him.

7

Ministering to Jesus

It had been a long day, and I was tired. I was tired of not getting enough sleep; tired of children needing me when all I wanted was to sit down and rest; tired of having so many things left to do on my list when the day was already mostly gone.

I wasn't in a very good mood as I prepared dinner. I don't like to cook, anyway, and being in a bad mood made the chore worse. Finally, supper was ready. I called the kids to the table as I fixed their plates in the kitchen (they were much younger at the time).

"Here," I said, carrying the plates into the dining room and slapping one down in front of the first kid.

"Mom, what's this?" the poor child asked innocently.

That did it. I'd had all I could take. "It's your supper," I said, forcing myself not to yell. "You can either eat it or not. But that's what you get."

There's nothing wrong with preparing only one meal and expecting your child to eat it if he or she wants supper. What was wrong was my attitude.

Would I have acted that way if I were serving Jesus? I asked myself. Then the thought hit me: I *was* serving Jesus. Jesus says that the way I serve my children is the way I serve Him. I felt bad enough about the way I had griped at my kids, but I felt even worse about the way I had just served my Lord.

• •

Jesus entrusts moms with children who are precious to Him, even more precious to Him than they are to us as moms. He entrusts them to our care to raise them for Him. What we invest in them is an offering to Him. —Elna B.

• •

That's the downside of the fact that our service is so significant. It's great that when we serve well, we have served Jesus well. But it's not so great that when we serve poorly, we serve Jesus poorly. Actually, there's a word for it. It's called *sin*.

The apostle Paul tells us in Colossians 3:23 that we are to do our work from our soul as unto the Lord rather than for men. That's because Paul knew that we have a higher standard when it comes to the Lord. We're willing to expend much more effort to render Him better service than we are for our family, our friends or anybody else. If we do everything as unto the Lord, that will be the best we can do it, and everybody else will benefit too. Hence the commandment.

I was doing my work from my soul, all right. My soul was not quiet and at peace. I was stressed. I was selfish. I was tired. I did the work with my own good in mind (which I defined as expending the least amount of effort possible), not with my children's good in mind, and certainly not with the Lord's. The first thing I should have done if I wanted to serve Jesus well was to make sure my soul was right. Right service can't come from a soul that's in the wrong place. A right soul has to come first if right service is to result.

How do you make sure your soul is in the right place?

The foundation is to spend regular time with the Lord. Not just time to ask Him for all the things on your list, but time to talk with Him. Time to praise Him, sing to Him, listen to Him, have fun with Him. Time to ask Him questions, and time simply to be together.

Most moms have difficulty finding regular quiet time to spend with God (including me!). If you are a single mom or a "single-ish" mom (such as when your husband is deployed for long periods of time), finding time alone is even harder. You don't have anyone who can take care of the kids while you take care of yourself. With time at a premium, how does a mom find time to care for her own soul?

Entire books have been written on that, but I'm just going to give you a couple of ideas here. They are the ideas that have made the most difference to me in my own spiritual walk and in the walks of those moms I know well.

First, as was the theme of my first book, get rid of the idea that your quiet time has to look a certain way. You don't have to sit down for a solid hour of just you and God in order to do it "right." In fact, there's no such thing as "right" as long as you are being obedient and coming before Him with a sincere heart. If you have long, uninterrupted blocks of time, by all means, take advantage of them! Even if you don't, try to plan one once in a while. In the meantime, relax. Realize that on some days, you'll only have five minutes by yourself, and that's okay. You have to learn to seize the time where you can.

It's too easy to get caught up in the day-to-day work of running a household and let quiet time with God fall by the wayside. If I miss my morning devotions, I won't get called out like I will if there aren't clean socks or I miss a deadline. I know that He has a way of multiplying my time when I put Him first, but it's still a daily struggle. —Carla L.

Fortunately, God is ready and willing to speak to you at any time. You don't have to get all your mommy tasks out of the way so that you can spend time with God; He can—and will—meet you right in the midst of them. In fact, He just may use the very ordinary things of your mothering, such as green bean plants, racquetballs, or wooden trains to speak to you and teach you His truth.

Your time with God will look different now than in the past, and that's okay. As long as you have time with Him, it doesn't have to fit into a certain format. In fact, a quote that I love puts it like this: "It took my not having an hour with Him to realize I had all day with Him."

What does spending all day with Him look like? We'll look at how it works out in four areas moms have to deal with often.

Mealtimes

"Uh, Mom? I didn't order this," Kenny said politely. He sat staring at the plate of food I set before him.

In his defense, sometimes when we have leftovers, we allow each child to come into the kitchen one at a time and choose what he or she would like to have for that meal. So it's understandable that Kenny would object on terms of not having "ordered" something. The only thing was that this time, I hadn't asked him.

● ●

Once, I went nine kinds of out of my way to make corn dog bites for Ryan in a desperate attempt to get him to eat. After a long prep and a slaving, hot cooking period, I put these in front of Ryan. My dear child, who had not yet spoken much of a sentence in his three-and-a-half years on this earth, said, "Can I have some dog food?" It's hilarious now, but it wasn't then!! —Crystal S.

● ●

Mealtimes are usually interesting in homes with young children. Whether it's your toddler who screams like you're trying to poison her with the same food she adored yesterday; your preschooler who accidentally knocks his entire plate of spaghetti and sauce onto the floor; two of your kids trying to see who can burp the loudest; or somebody feeding the dog under the table, there's usually something going on.

How can we make these times that are so vital to our family life an offering to Jesus as well as a way to spend time with Him? There are two primary ways.

First, cook and serve meals willingly. That seems obvious, but it can be hard, especially when you don't like to cook. Not liking to cook is okay (thank goodness). But complaining about cooking isn't okay. When you slam cabinet doors, flop meat onto the counter to be prepared or jerk pans out of the cupboard, you're making it clear that you don't really want to be doing what you're doing. Would you accept this kind of attitude from your kids? I don't think so. I know I wouldn't. We require our kids to do what they're told with a good attitude. We should do no less.

What do you think it communicates to your children or your husband when you make it obvious that you don't want to cook for them? It shows that you resent having to meet their needs. Is that what you want to show them, or worse, show Jesus? That you don't really have any desire to meet His needs and are only doing it because you have to?

So when you prepare meals, do it willingly. Make meal preparation a cheerful time. Even if you don't enjoy the task itself, you can still focus on the opportunity to serve your family, and you can enjoy that. If you can't be glad about the opportunity, take that to God. He will help change your heart.

Second, be creative. This doesn't mean that you have to serve a new and different meal every day. It doesn't mean you have to fold everybody's napkin into the shape of a swan. What it means is simply this: Think of ways to delight your family with the meals you serve. This may not always be possible (especially if you are serving something not all of them like). But often, it is possible.

You can be creative by serving their favorite food, serving dessert first, or cutting their sandwiches into shapes. You can make pancakes in the shape of the letters of their name; you can put fresh flowers or an interesting centerpiece on the table; you might even have a craft-making session where everyone makes his or her own placemat, which you then laminate. The exact way you demonstrate creativity doesn't matter. It will be different for each family. By using creativity every once in a while, you show your family that you care about making mealtimes a pleasant experience. You show them you're willing to put effort into doing something they need. And you encourage mealtimes to become fun-filled times rather than merely utilitarian.

They won't remember all of the different ways you showed creativity. But they will remember that you cared about serving their meals. And Jesus will remember that you cared about serving His.

Bathtime

Did you know that bath time can be a ton of fun? I didn't either, for a good long while. I was too caught up in the logistics of getting bath time done efficiently with so many small children who couldn't completely bathe themselves. I hated bath time.

I don't now. In fact, I like it. Why? Because I've realized that you can have a lot of fun during bath time. After all, does it really matter whether water gets sloshed over the side of the tub? Not really. All it takes is an extra towel to clean it up. Does it matter that baths took too long one night? No. Start earlier next time. It's not a big deal. The point is, have fun.

Why does having fun during bath time matter? Because it shows your kids that you enjoy taking care of them and that you're willing to let them have a little fun, even if it sometimes makes more work for you. It shows them that you know that even the routine things in life can be enjoyed.

What a great gift you give your children when you teach them that fun can be found even in the most ordinary parts of the day and when you help them have fun. You serve them—and Jesus—by providing fun for them and by teaching them the lifelong skill of finding fun in ordinary places.

. . . .

My youngest one loved bath time, and he loved to use scented soaps and shampoos. He said he smelled like a peach or an apple. For whatever reason, I always remember it. —Lilya B.

. . . .

Playtime

"Mommy? Would you wike to pway a game wif me?" Jessica's small voice asked. Her green eyes looked up at me hopefully.

I was busy. I was working on the computer on something I had to get done. I didn't have time to play.

On the other hand, I didn't have time not to.

I left my work and played with Jessica for two reasons: First, because she wanted me to; second, because I know the time is coming all too soon when she won't invite me to play with me nearly as much anymore. I don't want that time to come sooner than it has to. I don't want her to stop asking just because Mommy always says no. I want her to have the reasonable expectation that if at all possible, Mommy will play with her when she asks. Why? Because I want her to know that I care about being with her.

Whether you work outside the home or are a stay-at-home mom, there will be some days when you are simply too tired to play or the events of the day (or maybe lack of sleep the night before) have left you weary. There may be times when it's best to say, "Sweetheart, Mommy needs to rest right now. But after supper (or whatever other time would work), Mommy will play with you."

Children understand this. They know they can't always have what they want, including their mom's attention. Even though they might be disappointed at the moment, they can easily deal with this when you are only occasionally too busy or tired. It's when your usual answer is *no*—that no matter what or when they ask, Mommy isn't available—that they begin to feel they don't matter to you.

It's vital to your children's sense of self and sense of security to know that you want to spend time with them—that you're interested in their pursuits and want to join them in what they do (even though you may not be quite as enamored of their activities as they are, especially if they involve bugs or crawly things).

• •

I watch HGTV a lot and have it on sometimes when I'm feeding my daughter. One show I've gotten into lately is "Love It or List It." When the show is almost over, the couple in the show has to decide whether to love their renovated home and stay there or list it for sale. At that point, I look at Cara and say quickly in a funny voice, "Cara, love it or list it? Love it or list it? Love it or list it?" Cara absolutely squeals and laughs. There must be something hilarious about those words and how I say them! —Christi B.

• •

When your children feel that you care about them enough to be with them as often as you can, they will feel important to you.

In a previous chapter, we talked about how God is always available to you. Even though you can't always be available to your children, by making it a point to be willing to play with them and to show interest in their activities, you communicate to them that they matter. They are important to you. And you communicate the same thing to Jesus.

Bedtime

My husband and I sometimes liken bedtime to the game Whac-A-Mole. You know, it's the game where moles take turns popping up out of their little holes and you're supposed to push each one back down with a giant mallet before the next one pops up. We don't use a mallet at bedtime, but we do indeed have to put our children to bed repeatedly on some nights. It's amazing how often they need a drink after they're already in bed, or need to come tell us they love us, or develop sudden fears of the dark or want to tattle on somebody.

Bedtime can be a little bit crazy sometimes. It can also be a whole lot special.

Whether you have a certain routine you do every night or you thrive on spontaneity instead of routine, you can do something each night to make bedtime special. It can be something as simple as praying for your children or speaking a blessing over them as you put them in bed, or buying them fun kid toothpaste. Whatever you do, the point of making bedtime special is to help your children be at peace as they end their day and drift off to sleep.

What an incredible gift it is to allow your child to end the day peacefully, with a goodnight kiss or brushing her hair back from her forehead. What a privilege for a child to be able to go to bed knowing that he is loved and all is well in his home! A child who regularly has peaceful bedtimes (and yes, loud and crazy-fun bedtimes can put a child's soul at peace too) will feel secure. Security is one of the things I most want to give my children, and I know you feel the same way about yours.

So tonight, let your child's (or children's) bedtime be peaceful. Offer her—and Jesus—security and a good night's rest.

Following the evening ritual of my children getting a bath, having a snack and brushing their teeth before bedtime, I would tuck each child in bed. Most of the time we would talk a while, then have prayer and say goodnight. It was a special time to be alone with each child. —Elna B.

Whatever ways you choose to make these and other areas of daily life special for your children, you can be sure that by doing so, you are showing your children you love them. Ultimately, that is the greatest thing you can do in serving them. Show your children you love them by the manner in which you serve them, and you will be showing Jesus the same thing. Your children will be grateful, and so will He.

Going Deeper

Do you serve your family from a willing heart? If you struggle in this area, confess your struggle to God. If you don't, ask Him to keep your heart always willing.

8

Working in Jesus

Math isn't Ellie's strong suit. She can do it, but she doesn't like it. This is partly because math doesn't come easily to her.

I remember a time when I was trying to teach Ellie a particular math concept. She wasn't getting it. "This is hard!" she said.

"School is hard work sometimes," I replied.

She turned to me and said matter-of-factly, "But you know I don't like to work."

Indeed. Work isn't always fun. Not for her, and not for anyone else either, including moms.

Sometimes the task isn't fun. Who really enjoys doing laundry? (If you do, please come to my house and help me take care of mine!) Sometimes the task is fun but hard. (Taking kids to a carnival, anyone?) Other times, not only is the task less than fun, but it's also hard, such as when you're cleaning up potty training accidents on the same day you have to get the house cleaned because your in-laws are coming for a visit, which also happens to be the same day you have to do the grocery shopping, pick up a prescription from the drugstore and take the cat to the vet.

Then there are the mommy tasks that are even harder: figuring out how to discipline a child who won't stop back talking; comforting a child who got made fun of at school and never wants to go back; and explaining to your child why she can't play with a certain friend anymore.

Being a mommy is *hard*, both physically and emotionally. It's easy to get worn down without even realizing it's happening until it's too late and you realize you're about to hit bottom. Moms have to give and give and give; it's part of their job. And it takes a toll on us. Even the strongest, best-put-together, most well-organized mom will have her moments when she feels depleted. It's inevitable.

• •

One of the most difficult things about being a mother is that you
can never be doing just one thing at a time. You become the
"doer" of everything for everyone. For example, I'm trying to
pack lunches, but I have to stop to change a diaper; while I'm
changing that diaper, my older two get into an argument. Then
while I'm dealing with that, the youngest loses her socks. Eventually, I get back to lunches. Never being able to finish one task at
a time is mentally exhausting! —Kirstie F.

• •

Society tells us that when we feel depleted, we need to take better care of ourselves. Granted, a mom absolutely needs to take care
of herself, both because she's a person, too, and so that she will
have something left to give to those under her care. Taking care of
ourselves is a good answer, but it's not the best answer. That's because taking better care of ourselves by pampering ourselves more
or getting more alone time will help, but it won't do the full job.
There's only one answer that will, and society won't tell you that,
because it doesn't realize the value of the answer.

What's the answer? Work in Jesus' strength and with His abilities.

We hear that phrase all the time—"in His strength." We're supposed to do things "in His strength." But what does that actually
mean? What does it look like to do things in Jesus' strength and
not in our own? And what difference does it make, anyway?

How to Work in Jesus' Strength

First, let's clarify something. Working in Jesus' strength doesn't
mean you will never get tired or need sleep. When Jesus walked on
this earth, He got tired plenty of times. In fact, one time He was so
tired that He was able to sleep in a boat that was pitching around
and about to sink because of a storm (see Matt. 8:24). Jesus knew
what it was to be tired, having fully given Himself to the work of
His ministry.

Yet even when He was exhausted; even when the people were
pressing upon Him from all sides and He must have been tired;

even when He felt just plain *wiped out*, His soul was at rest. That's what working in His strength means: not that you will never feel weary, but that your work doesn't take away from the peace of your soul. When your soul isn't at peace, that's when you know you are trying with your own strength. Jesus will give us the physical strength we need in order to carry out His work; but even better than that, He will give us soul strength—strength of mind, heart, spirit and emotions.

We ask for physical strength, and that is good, but our request is too small. We should be asking for an abundance of soul strength. It's not physical strength that will enable us to be patient with our kids for the umpteenth time (though being well-rested certainly helps); it's soul strength. Likewise, it's not merely physical rest that helps us pour love into our children, but soul rest.

• •

Finding soul rest in the midst of exhaustion? Music based on Scripture does it hands down for me. —Cara B.

• •

There have been times when my body was worn out completely and I felt like I had nothing left to give. Then a child would come to me with a need, and somehow I would find strength to meet that need. The difference between whether I did so willingly or resentfully, fully or from a position of feeling empty, had to do with the state of my soul.

"Come unto Me"

We've all heard the passage that begins "Come unto Me . . . ," where Jesus speaks of giving us rest. I suspect that many of us have thought, *Well, that's nice, but I'm still really exhausted all the time.* Again, Jesus didn't promise that we would never feel physically tired; He promised that our souls would find rest in Him. So when we look for a kind of rest that He is not promising, we conclude that His words don't really work—or maybe they do for someone else, but not for us. But when we seek the kind of rest He's offering, we find not only that His words apply to us, but that we receive abundantly more than we thought we would, and that the rest He does provide reaches into every corner of our lives.

Let's look at this passage in the book of Matthew more closely.

Come to me, all who labor and are heavy laden, and I will give you rest. Take my yoke upon you, and learn from me, for I am gentle and lowly in heart, and you will find rest for your souls. For my yoke is easy, and my burden is light (Matt. 11:28-30).

Whether you are single or married; whether you are a teenager or in your—ahem—forties, like me; whether you have one child or five, you will be busy. You will have a lot of work to do. And if you don't take Jesus' yoke upon you, you will make your yoke harder than it has to be. After all, He says that His yoke is easy and his burden is light.

Let's see how that works.

"Come unto me, all who labor and are heavy laden"

Does this apply to moms, or what? Do we indeed labor, and are we often heavy laden with tasks that simply must be accomplished? Yep. Every one of us.

My first four children were born pretty close together. In fact, my oldest, Ellie, was still four when Jessica, my fourth child, was born. Whenever we were out in public, people would see me pushing a stroller with a baby and toddler riding in it and another toddler and a preschooler walking alongside. They would look back and forth from me to the kids and say something like, "Are all these yours?"

"Yes, they are," I would say with a smile.

It was the same response every time. "Wow, you sure have your hands full." Now that I have five children, even though they range in age from ten years to one year, it seems that I get that comment equally often.

"You sure have your hands full." Indeed. But truly, every mom has her hands full, whether you have 1 child or 10. This is especially true if you are a single mom. You don't have a built-in helper living in your home. Childcare duties fall squarely upon your shoulders even more than they do upon the average mom's, because there's just you.

Okay, so we qualify: we labor, and we're heavy laden. That means Jesus is talking to us when He invites, "Come unto me." But just what exactly does coming to Him mean?

• •

I hate to say this, but oftentimes I don't see Jesus in the everyday things. Life with many children gets so hectic at times that it's just about all I can do to make it through the day on automated mode—going from one activity to the next as if life depended on the mundane tasks of the day being completed. But then Jesus breaks through in the Bible verse that stands out in my quiet time addressing some pressing need; the kindness of one child to another; or a song on the radio or a word aptly spoken that brings me before the throne of grace. Sometimes it is just a look out the window to see the branches of the trees in the yard swaying in the wind, knowing that there is a force behind the movement that I cannot see. The unseen hand of God that sways the branches can meet all of my needs too. I guess that those are the things that show me Jesus in everyday life. —Marilee B.

• •

First, it means that we seek Him regularly. We need to have regular time with God. Whether that means we talk to Him while we shower or actually have a sit-down time where we can read our Bible and pray, we need to make it a point to come to Him. And when we do—wherever, whenever that is—we need to be prepared both to talk and to listen.

Yes, God dearly wants to hear from us. He also wants to speak to us. Our time with Him should not be merely a time to "upload" all of our requests and things we have to say. It should consist of more than just saying, "Dear God, please bless this and this and this, and please help that person, and thank you for all Your many blessings. Amen," and then going about our work.

In other words, yes, absolutely pour out your heart to God, including your problems, requests and thoughts. But don't make it a monologue where He's expected to listen and then do something about it while you go on your merry way. Tell Him what you have to say, but then listen to what He has to say. You probably won't hear an audible voice, but you may hear Him in your spirit. There have even been times when my children spoke words that I knew were a message from God to me. Don't worry about how He will communicate with you. He knows how to get through to you. But that assumes that you are listening.

"… and I will give you rest."

Notice the third word: "will." Not *might. Will.* When we come to Jesus, we can come in full assurance that we will receive the rest we ask for. For me, and maybe for you, that's incredible. I well remember a time in my life when I didn't ask God for very much because I figured He would probably say no to most of it. Rather than risk a no, which I would have seen as rejection of me personally, I just didn't ask for much of anything.

But rest? I can feel confident asking for that! God says that He *will* do it, and He never lies, forgets or changes His mind. The only caveat is that I must come believing and not doubting, because Scripture also commands us to "ask in faith, with no doubting, for the one who doubts is like a wave of the sea that is driven and tossed by the wind. For that person must not suppose that [she] will receive anything from the Lord; [she] is a double-minded [mom], unstable in all [her] ways" (Jas. 1:6-8, adapted).

That's not to say that if I somehow muster up enough belief, I can obligate God to give me what I want. The only things God will give me are those that are in accordance with His perfect will.

But this verse clearly states that when you come to Him, He *will* give you rest. You *will* get it—though He gets to choose the details.

"Take my yoke upon you"

A yoke is something that hitches two animals, often oxen, together so that they can work together. The oxen work side by side, and what they do together is greater than what they can do separately, because they are yoked.

Jesus isn't talking about wearing a wooden yoke here. He's talking about taking on a bond—being bound together with Him to work together. He wants you to take on *His* yoke, not someone else's, and not your own. We are not to bind ourselves to someone who doesn't know how to direct the work of our lives—society, for example, or a teacher of false doctrine. Neither are we to attempt to do the work alone, with the other half of our yoke empty, trying to fulfill both roles. We need someone in the other half, and that Someone should be Jesus. We are to join ourselves to Him and work together.

The fact that Jesus speaks about "taking" His yoke upon us means that we have to be willing. He will not force Himself on you. He's given you a choice whether to do things His way or not. If you choose to leave the other half of your yoke empty or fill it with someone besides Jesus, He'll let you do it. It will be your own fault that you struggle in your work, because you aren't yoked to the right Person.

"Learn from me"

Are you willing to learn? Are you teachable? Or do you tend to tell Jesus the way things should be done?

Consider your prayer time. Do you spend more time telling Jesus what you want Him to bless or asking for His thoughts on those matters? When a difficulty or new situation arises in your life, do you try to figure it out on your own, with maybe some advice from girlfriends or self-help books, without ever consulting Jesus? If so, you may not be very teachable.

When you come to Jesus, you have to be willing to learn from Him. Coming to Him and trying to force Him to carry out your desires is hardly the kind of "coming" He's talking about. Be willing to be taught of Him. Be willing to see things a different way. You already know that Jesus' ways are different from yours. You need to trust that not only are they different, but they're far better.

• •

The times that I fail the most miserably are the times when I do not weigh the counsel I am given by those around me against the instructions given to me by my Lord. In Matthew 22, we are told to, "Love the Lord your God with all your heart and with all your soul and with all your mind." Also to, "Love your neighbor as yourself" (Matt. 22:37-39, *NIV*). When I weigh my thoughts and actions against these two Scriptures in particular, very often the answer to my struggles becomes abundantly clear. Love God, love others. —Marilee B.

• •

"... for I am gentle and lowly in heart ..."

Here, Jesus is telling us what kind of Master He is. He's not a brutish dictator who will force you to bend to His every whim. Yes, He is absolutely the Lord of all Creation. Yet He is extending you an invitation, not commanding you. He will allow you to make the choice. If you don't want to come to a Master like Him, you are free to choose somebody else. Why you'd want to do that, I don't know, because nobody, including yourself, can come anywhere close to having the kind of loving, gentle heart that Jesus has.

"... and you will find rest for your souls."

See? He's telling us again. He wants to make sure we understand what He's offering. He wants to make sure we know that rest is a certainty, not a possibility. He's graciously telling us one more time in case we've forgotten or weren't sure He meant it the first time— or in case we were so awed by His offer that we simply couldn't comprehend it by only hearing it once.

"For my yoke is easy, and my burden is light"

I'll admit that this part of the verse has been the most difficult part for me to understand. Perhaps you've wondered the same thing:

How can Jesus say that His yoke is easy and His burden is light when it sure doesn't feel that way? When I'm constantly work, work, working, and hardly ever get to rest; when the circumstances of my life are so difficult; when—well, have You seen my children?!

Yes, Jesus has seen your children. Yes, He has seen your husband, if you are married. Yes, He has seen the burden of doing it all yourself, if you're single. Yes, Jesus has seen every difficult aspect of your life. And yet He still tells you that His yoke is easy and His burden is light. How can this be?

The answer is found in the meaning of the original Greek word. The Greek term that is used here to mean "easy" doesn't mean "easy" as in the opposite of "difficult." It means "easy" as in the opposite of "harsh."

Jesus never promises that being yoked together with Him won't be difficult. In fact, we read in James 1:2, "Count it all joy, my brothers, *when* you meet trials of various kinds" (emphasis added). Clearly, we are going to have trials and troubles. That's certain. So Jesus is not saying that His yoke will necessarily be the opposite of difficult. He's saying that it will be the opposite of harsh.

What is the opposite of harsh? "Easy" is one possible translation. But another possible translation, which I believe gives a better idea of what Jesus is actually talking about, is "gentle." Jesus is saying that the yoke He puts on us will be gentle. It won't be designed to hurt, harass or intimidate us. It will be restful and soothing. That's because when we yoke ourselves to Jesus, we can find rest for our souls in the fact that Jesus is in charge. He knows everything; He's all-powerful; and He will take care of everything. Rest for our souls, like we talked about earlier. See how it all works together?

Now, when Jesus says that His burden is light, "light" means exactly what we think it means—the opposite of "heavy." And a burden, of course, is something that Jesus has asked us to carry. So, again, we get back to the question, "Light? Really? Have You seen my circumstances?"

Yes, Jesus has seen your circumstances. He's well aware that they might be difficult. Yet, He still says that what He's asked you to carry isn't heavy, but light. What does He mean?

Simply this, precious mom: Sometimes we take more upon ourselves than what Jesus ever meant for us to carry.

See if any of the following ideas has ever gotten stuck in your head (or may be stuck there right now):

I should be able to take care of my kids as well as keep my house clean all the time.

I should be full of creative ideas for helping my children to learn and to have fun so there is never a dull moment around my house.

I should always be able to be patient and kind with my kids, no matter whether I've had any sleep or not; no matter whether I'm sick or not; no matter whether I'm at my wits' end or not.

I should never need to use the television as a babysitter just so I can get a shower.

I should always serve delicious, nutritious meals. Serving frozen chicken nuggets more than one night a week is a sign of failure.

Does any of these scenarios sound familiar to you? Maybe more than one? Sometimes we grab hold of a false idea and accept it as gospel, placing a burden on ourselves that Jesus never meant for us to carry. These are *our* burdens, not His.

• •

I think there is a lot of perceived pressure to keep up with what we think other moms are achieving. My house is a disaster, and it's embarrassing. But with a full-time job and three kids, obsessive neatness just isn't possible. I think we really can't have it all. Something has to give, and you have to decide what those sacrifices will be. —Kirstie F.

• •

But what about the "burden" Jesus has asked me, personally, to carry? He's asked me to be a wife, a mother to five kids, a homemaker and a homeschool teacher. How can He say that's a light burden?

He never asked me to do those things perfectly. He only asked me to do my best. *I'm* the one who places the burden of perfectionism on myself. *I'm* the one who sees "my best" as "not good enough" unless it produces the results I'm hoping for. Being the perfect wife, mom and homemaker? Not possible. A "heavy" burden. But being the best one I can be, and trusting that the results of my best efforts will be good enough for Jesus? Yes. Possible. A "light" burden.

Do you feel relieved to know that all Jesus expects from you is your best, and He will be responsible for the results? I do. And I'm grateful for such a kind, gentle Savior who won't ask of me more than I can do, and who calls me only to do the best I can with what He's given me. He is a Savior who imposes light burdens, indeed.

But an easy yoke and a light burden aren't the only motherhood-related gifts we receive from Jesus, even as incredible as they are. He has all kinds of rewards planned for us, if we just know where to look for them, as we will see in the next chapter.

Going Deeper

Do you need to learn to work in God's strength instead of your own? Ask Him to teach you how. Do you place burdens on yourself that Jesus never meant for you to carry? Ask Him to show you, and if He points out one (or more), release it to Him.

9

Receiving from Jesus

Beside my bed hangs a piece of artwork. It consists of a piece of printer paper on which the artist—then four-year-old Lindsey—attached a 4-inch square piece of material and carefully printed, "You are a great mommy."

Some of the letters are backwards, and some of the words are spelled wrong. But that artwork is beyond precious to me. Lindsey presented it to me one day, carrying it carefully into my room in her little hands. "I made this for you," she said. "It's so if you ever feel discouraged or have a bad day, you can look at it." I carefully sounded out the words, and my heart melted.

I embraced Lindsey and thanked her, though my words seemed inadequate, at least to me. Then she and I went to a nearby store and picked out a frame for it. I let Lindsey choose. The frame she chose is silver, textured and shiny. She thinks it's beautiful, and so do I. When we got home, I put her gift into the frame and hung it by my bed where I can see it every day. Lindsey was quietly overjoyed at the way I received her gift, and I made sure to tell her several times in the days and weeks following that I had looked at her gift that day. Each time, she would smile. Sometimes she would throw her arms around me. But I'm convinced that I received far more than she did.

That picture will hang beside my bed forever, because it's a beautiful expression of my daughter's heart toward me, and it encourages my heart every time I see it.

But it's not just from Lindsey. It's from Jesus too.

• •

Two years ago, right before Christmas, I was bustling around cooking, wrapping and trying to get ready for [Christmas] festivities. I still had several kids at home, but the married

ones were coming over, too, and things were pretty busy.
When all the kids got to the house, it seemed like they kept
disappearing instead of helping me, or at least hanging out with
me. It was a really busy time, and I kept thinking, *Where is everybody?* Later, I found out. When we opened gifts, there was a big
one for me. It was a large photo collage that my youngest
daughter had put together; in addition to photos of all my kids,
including daughters-in-law, it also had a note of appreciation
from each one. I don't cry easily, but I cried as I looked at that
gift covered with pictures and words of love and thankfulness
from my family. That picture hangs over my desk in my bedroom;
every time I see it, I'm reminded that after all those crazy, busy
and often unappreciated times, there's an awesome reward that
comes from being a mom. —Melisa N.

Recognizing Our Children's Affirmation

We talked in a previous chapter about how our children can't completely fill our appreciation cup. That's true; they're human beings, and young ones, at that. But we need to realize that our
children do give us far more affirmation than we are probably
aware of. In this chapter, we'll learn how to recognize our children's affirmation for what it is.

When I received Lindsey's gift, her affirmation was obvious to
me. After all, it said, right there on the page, "You are a great
mommy." As a matter of fact, Lindsey frequently initiates telling
me that I'm the best mommy ever, or that she loves me "sooooooo
much." I feel so blessed to have her in my life, because virtually
every day, she affirms and appreciates me. (She's even been known
to say, unprompted, "Thank you for making my supper.")

My other kids tell me they love me too. (Well, Timmy doesn't,
but since he's a baby, I will excuse him.) Your children probably
do the same. But if we only realize they're affirming us when they're
actually saying it, we're going to miss a whole lot of affirmation we
could be soaking in otherwise.

Let's look at several of the common ways our children affirm us, which we often miss.

"Mommy, I Need ..."

If I had a dollar for every time I heard a sentence beginning with "Mommy, I need ..." I would be rich. You probably would too. Children are needy people. There are many things they know how to do for themselves but can't, because they're not yet physically able; there are many things they don't yet know how to do. (Of course, there are also the things they know perfectly well how to do and just don't feel like doing because they're being lazy, but that's not what we're talking about here.)

Have you ever realized that when they come to you for your help, they are affirming you?

I hadn't realized it until recently. I confess that sometimes, especially on days when I'm feeling particularly depleted, I get annoyed at my children's constant needs. It's not that they're doing anything wrong; they're only being kids. I have no reason to be annoyed except for being selfish (which is a bad reason). Never before had I thought of my children's requests for help as affirmations. But I do now.

Now, when they say, "Mommy, I need ..." I realize they're also saying one or more of the following:

"Mommy, I know you have the ability to do it."

"You're a caring mommy. I know you care about helping me."

"I look up to you, Mommy. You can do things I can't."

Why in the world do I choose to hear something annoying in their constant requests when I could be hearing constant praise of my abilities as a mom and constant reminders that they trust me to care?

I bet it will make an incredible difference in how I respond to their requests when I learn to hear the affirmation instead of the inconvenience. Maybe it would make a difference for you too.

"Mommy, My Brother (Sister) Bothered Me"

If you're like me, refereeing sibling squabbles tops the list of "Really Annoying Things to Do That Should Never Have Gotten This Far."

I hate having to mediate a dispute about something that doesn't really matter. But I bet my perspective on this unpleasant mothering task would be different if I heard the affirmation in what my kids were saying instead of merely the tattling:

"Mommy, I know you care about what's right and what's wrong. You are a just person."

"Mommy, you've taught me well. I care about what's right and wrong too."

"Mommy, I know you will make the right decision in this matter."

"Mommy, I know you care when I've been mistreated."

Granted, deciding who was at fault in the untimely demise of a Lego creation may never be your favorite thing to do. But it wouldn't be quite so bad if you could also hear the affirmation in addition to the tattling.

"Mommy, I Peed in My Bed" (or Any Other Unpleasant Situation)

When my child confesses something such as wetting the bed, my first thought is not that she has just affirmed me. My first thought is usually about the inconvenience this will mean for me. Know what I mean? Maybe instead of thinking about the fact that we're going to have to change the sheets—*again*—we should hear one or more of the following affirmations:

"Mommy, I know you still love and accept me, even when I tell you something you don't want to hear."

"Mommy, you've taught me not to hide my mistakes. See? I've learned the lesson."

"Mommy, I trust you to handle this situation right and to handle me gently, even though we both know I've done something you wish I hadn't."

How might hearing our child's affirmation make a difference in the way we respond verbally? In the attitude with which we go change the sheets? In the way we grumble to ourselves about how this child will *never* be potty-trained?

I bet we wouldn't grumble nearly so much. We might even be thankful for the opportunity to receive this affirmation.

Your Child Crawls into Your Bed in the Middle of the Night

For quite some time, while she was three years old, Jessica would make a nightly appearance at my side of the bed. "Can I sweep wif you?" she would ask.

I'd scoot over and allow her to "spoon" next to me, covering her with the comforter and snuggling her close. Long before I got back to sleep, she was asleep.

After missing enough sleep due to having her in bed with me (she's also wiggly when she sleeps), I began to get annoyed. Until, that is, I realized that all too soon, those days would be gone, and Jessica wouldn't be crawling into my bed anymore. Suddenly, those nights became precious to me, and I was more than willing to trade part of a night's sleep for memories I'd remember the rest of my life.

I'll bet my realization would have come even sooner had I known that when Jessica came into my room, she wasn't just looking for a new place to sleep, she was also saying:

"Mommy, when I'm lonely, there's no place I'd rather be than with you."

"Mommy, when the world is big and dark and scary, I'm most comforted by being with you."

"Mommy, when I'm with you, I can be at peace."

Your Child Snuggles into Your Lap While You Watch TV

Usually, we find this experience pleasant. We all enjoy cuddling with our kids on the couch while we watch a favorite program. I bet we'd enjoy it even more if we realized they were saying far more than, "May I sit here?"

"Mommy, when I'm having a great day, I want to celebrate by being with you."

"Mommy, life is more fun when I'm with you."

"Mommy, I love you. There's no place else I'd rather be."

Who can resist cuddling a child who's saying all those things? Even if they talk a little bit too much during the program, so what? You may not hear all the words on the TV, but you have heard all of your child's affirmations.

For bedtime, we like to do our Bible studies—not every
night, but we do it, and after that the kids will watch one
movie and go to sleep. —Amanda M.

Your Child Brings You Some Kind of Artwork or Creation

I've already shared my story of the time when Lindsey brought me
her picture, and how affirmed I felt. But affirmation comes even
when it's not obvious. Hear what your child is saying when he or
she brings you something special:

"Mommy, I love you, so I want to give you something, and this
is what I have."

"Mommy, I want you to have something, and I care enough
that you have something that I'm willing to spend my time making it for you."

"Mommy, I trust you to affirm me by showing that you like
what I've made."

"Mommy, words fail me to express my love for you, so I'm giving you this gift."

"Watch Me!"

Jessica likes doing what she calls "tricks," which usually involve
some sort of physical feat, such as jumping from the coffee table
to the floor. Often, Lindsey accompanies her, and they put on a
show together (for which they usually charge $1 admittance. It's
well worth it).

Kenny likes to show me that he can now do what he's been working on in his gymnastics class. Occasionally, Ellie will do the same.

But when my children ask me to watch them do something,
they're not merely offering to let me see something they can do.
They're also saying:

"Mommy, I know you rejoice with me when I can do something well. Thanks!"

"Mommy, I love it when you're proud of me. Your approval
means so much."

"Mommy, I feel so good when you tell me I've done well. Thanks for building me up."

"Mommy, I know that when I have a need for affirmation, I can come to you. You are always faithful to affirm me."

See what I mean? If we hear not only our children's actual words but also the words they're too young to know how to say, we'll hear affirmation and praise from them all day long. It's our choice, moms. Do we want to be annoyed all day long, or do we want to be built up? Let's listen to what our children are really saying—not just with their words but with their actions. Let's not miss what they're telling us with their hearts.

Let's also not fail to realize one important thing, perhaps the most vitally important thing of all: When our children affirm us, that same affirmation is also coming from Jesus.

Receiving Affirmation From Jesus

Have you ever felt prompted to give someone a compliment or say something encouraging, and you did, and it made a big difference in that person's day? You felt better, and the other person felt better. Both of you were blessed.

That's what I'm talking about. Often, Jesus will prompt us to step into someone's life and touch him or her in a very real and tangible way so that he or she can be encouraged. Jesus knows that person needs a touch that day, and He gives us the privilege of partnering with Him to make a difference in that person's life.

Jesus does the same in our children. He knows just how to bond parents and children together. He knows that parents need affirmation from children, and He arranges for it—not against our children's wills, but as natural expressions of the precious little people they are.

So any praise or affirmation we receive from our children comes, in this way, from Jesus. But it's also from Jesus in another way.

Remember how I said that Jesus takes our actions toward our children personally? That whatever we do to and for our children, we do to and for Him?

....

Tonya G. tells of a time when she wanted a song downloaded by
a specific artist but had never heard the particular song. When
she asked her 13-year-old son to download the song by this
artist, he refused to download that particular song and told her
he didn't think she needed to listen to that kind of music. After
listening to the song for herself, she realized the foul language
that was used, and she knew she had taught her son well.

....

Jesus feels the same appreciation and praise our children feel
(though several times greater, of course, because He is perfect and
perfectly mature, and He understands just how hard it is to get up
in the middle of the night for the fourth time). Our children appreciate us for being trustworthy toward them; Jesus appreciates
us for being trustworthy to Him. Our children are grateful when
we take the time to comfort them; Jesus is thankful when we take
the time to comfort *Him*.

When you look at it this way—that almost everything your
children say to you is an affirmation and that Jesus is saying the
same thing—you begin to realize that you're not quite as lacking
for affirmation as you thought you were. Not anywhere close. Instead of feeling like your cup is empty, you can feel full all day—
even when nobody's saying anything, because you know that Jesus
appreciates you all the time and that His Holy Spirit will confirm
it in your heart any time you need to hear it.

Going Deeper

How have your children affirmed you today? How has God affirmed you? Thank Him for the affirmation He pours into your
life and ask Him to help you not miss it.

_____

_____

_____

1 0

Resting in Jesus

Recently, I conducted a non-random, completely unscientific poll among my FB friends and those who have "liked" my author page. The question was this: *Do you get enough sleep?*

The answer choices were:

A. Sure, all the time.
B. Usually
C. Every now and then, if I'm lucky.
D. Almost never
E. Hahahahahahahaha!

Among parents, choice E won by a mile, as I had the sneaking suspicion it would. (By the way, if your answer was A, and you have young children, *you* need to write a book for the rest of us to tell us how to do it!)

The point is, we don't get the rest we need on a regular basis.

If you were hoping this chapter would be about how to get your kids to sleep better so that you can sleep better, you may be disappointed. But I don't think so. In this chapter, we are indeed going to look at the issue of rest, but at a far deeper level than just whether or not we get a good night's sleep (though we'll touch on that). So hang in there!

How Important Is Sleep?

I thought we should address this question right off. After all, it's vitally important to most moms. Not too long after I had my son Timmy (who is now four months old), my sister asked me, "So, are you getting enough sleep?"

I told her that Timmy sleeps reasonably well for his age, but that no, I couldn't remember the last time I had a full eight hours.

"I always ask," my sister said, "because that's really the only thing that matters to new moms."

Of course she was exaggerating, but not much!

When my first daughter, Ellie, was born, she was an excellent sleeper. From day one, she would sleep four hours at a time, wake up, eat, then go back to sleep for another four. By eight weeks, she was sleeping through the night (eight hours) every single night.

I remember being so spoiled in regard to her sleep patterns that I actually complained to my husband—wait for it—that I had to go to bed immediately after Ellie did, or I might only get 7.5 hours of sleep. Yeah, I know. I'm shaking my head too.

So right up until Kenny, my second child, was born, I failed to understand why people complained so much about babies not sleeping through the night. I thought maybe everybody else just got "bad sleeper" babies or something.

Little did I know that everybody else had average, ordinary babies in terms of sleep, and that my subsequent children would sleep like those babies—or even worse.

The reason why rest matters so much to a mom is that without it, you and I can't entirely be the mom we want to be. Sometimes we can't even keep our eyes open during the day. We're more likely to be cranky and impatient. We're certainly less creative. We feel fogged over.

So, yes, it's definitely important to get a good night's sleep whenever you can. And the reason I'm devoting a section to sleep in this book is to encourage you to make sleep a priority.

But I already do, you say. *At least, I try. It just never works!*

If you truly do make sleep a priority, then feel free to skip this section. But it's possible that you don't make sleep a priority even though you think you do.

For instance, after your kids go to bed, do you stay up another hour or two, cleaning the house before falling into bed exhausted?

But when else would I get anything done? you ask.

After the kids are in bed may very well be a good time to accomplish things. But it's also possible that if you used the time to get some extra sleep instead, you'd be more rested during the day and, therefore, more productive. You might even find more opportunities to get things done than you currently do, simply because you're so tired that you don't see them.

And what about physical rest during the day?

Now when would I ever get that? you ask.

Okay, I'm going to advocate something that in my pre-child days I never imagined I would want to do: It really is okay to use television for a babysitter sometimes. If you truly need a nap, there's nothing wrong with putting your kids in front of a video (approved by you, of course) and getting the sleep you need. Granted, unless you are pregnant or have a newborn, you probably shouldn't do this every day. But once in a while won't hurt. Put your need for rest in front of your pride or in front of the idea that a good mom never lets the TV babysit her kids. (Believe me, I know *lots* of good moms who do this on occasion.)

Not only that, but it's okay to sit down on the couch and rest, read a book or watch TV yourself sometimes. Your kids will not die if mommy is not an active playmate every second of the day.

Now, let me be clear: I'm not advocating laziness. But there are times when you will legitimately need rest or recreation. You need it. Your body needs it. Your children need for you to have it. So call a friend to watch the kids, sit down and let the housework wait (unfortunately, it will still be there when you get up), or just go sit on the front porch and let the kids play in the yard (we do this one a lot, except when it's 156 degrees, like it is here in the summer). Even Jesus Himself sometimes left tasks waiting and went off to get some rest, and He encouraged His disciples to do the same. So be discerning about when your need for rest is legitimate, and if it is, make it a priority.

Resting Physically in Jesus

Now that we've talked about physical rest, let's talk about the subject of this chapter—resting in Jesus. Sounds like a good idea. But what does it mean, anyway? And how do we do it?

Rest is something Jesus urges you to take and provides for you.

In Mark 6:31, Jesus and the disciples had just been doing a whole lot of ministry. Things were getting crazy. (Sound like your house at all?) "Then, because so many people were coming and going that they did not even have a chance to eat, [Jesus] said to them, 'Come with me by yourselves to a quiet place and get some rest'" (*NIV*).

Jesus knows that you need rest. He made your body, remember? He knows you can't run on empty indefinitely. Needing rest isn't a sign of weakness; it isn't a sign of being a bad mom or of any such thing. It's simply a sign that your body is working the way Jesus made it to, and now it is time to get some of the rest He made it to need. Don't feel guilty that you can't keep going. Accept your body's need for rest as a reminder from Jesus, and do something about it.

Not only will Jesus remind you that you need to rest, but He will also provide rest for you. "In vain you rise early and stay up late, toiling for food to eat—for he grants sleep to those he loves" (Ps. 127:2, *NIV*). In other words, mom, don't run yourself ragged. If you do, it's in vain. Jesus is ready and willing to grant you the sleep you need—but He probably won't force you to slow down and take it.

But I don't get enough sleep, you say. True, sometimes Jesus may ask us to work on less sleep than we think we need—certainly less than we would like. But He knows the limits of your body, heart, mind and emotions better than you do. He will not deny you sleep when He knows you *truly* need it. He will never deny you any good thing.

It may not feel too good to run on "too little" sleep for too long, but life isn't all about feeling good. When Jesus says that you need sleep, sleep will be available—if you're willing to slow down, accept His reminder and do something about it.

Resting Spiritually in Jesus

Okay, so we talked about resting physically in Jesus. What about resting spiritually in Him? What does that mean?

It's like this: imagine you are holding your newborn baby in your arms. Your baby is fed, and his little tummy is full. He's feeling nice and warm, because you have him covered in a soft, fluffy blanket. His little eyelids get heavier and heavier, and finally close.

He's asleep. A few minutes later, the pacifier falls out of his little mouth, which stays open, but he doesn't even twitch.

That baby is completely at rest. He feels relaxed and secure. He's not worried about whether you are going to drop him or forget about him. He knows you're right there, and that's all he needs.

So it is with you and Jesus. It's like lying in Jesus' arms, completely trusting, completely satisfied and completely relaxed. You're not worrying about whether He's going to drop you. You trust Him.

Do you have a relationship like that with Jesus? Maybe you've never met Him. If not, please contact me in one of the ways listed at the back of this book, and I'll be glad to introduce you to Him.

Or maybe you do have a relationship with Jesus, and sometimes it's like it should be, but sometimes (since, of course, you are a human being), it's not. Resting spiritually in Jesus means that you look to Him for your ultimate rest.

Believe it or not, physical rest is not the ultimate kind of rest. Lest you think I'm saying this because I get plenty of rest, let me tell you that the answer to my own poll from the beginning of the chapter was E. (Ha-ha-ha-ha-ha-ha-ha-ha!) It is possible to be spiritually at rest even when you are not physically at rest (good thing, too, or I'd be doomed to spiritual unrest for another 18 years or so).

Resting Emotionally in Jesus

One of the many great things about Jesus is that He will not only provide rest for your body and for your spirit, but also for your emotions. He cares about those too. He cares about how you feel in the midst of the calling placed on you, and He knows that emotions can wear you out. So He provides emotional rest too.

How? Two primary ways: by listening to you and by counseling you.

Sometimes, we get the idea that we can't share our emotions with Jesus because they might be unrighteous, and we shouldn't bring such things to Him. We should get our emotions right *before* we approach Him.

I'm not sure where this idea first came from, but it's baloney. Yes, we should always approach Jesus respectfully and with a sincere heart, but this doesn't mean that we can never bring negative emotions to Him. In fact, we read in Psalm 51, "Surely you desire truth in the inner parts; you teach me wisdom in the inmost place" (Ps. 51:6, *NIV*).

In other words, Jesus *wants* you to be truthful about how you feel. Not just because He doesn't want you to lie, but because He wants you to be free to share your emotions with Him so that He can respond to you.

This is how it works: You share your emotions with Him and He communicates back. He will teach you wisdom in the inmost place.

One day when I just couldn't take it ANYMORE—bills overflowing, with very limited income and my three boys so rowdy and rambunctious (like always) that life was just getting to me—I had my husband watch the boys long enough for me to take a nice, relaxing, much needed bubble bath in a quiet, candlelit bathroom. As I prepared my hot bath, I made sure to include my Bible with the washcloth and towel. I read a passage by candlelight that spoke volumes to me! It reminded me that I have so much. Things may get tough sometimes, but God gave me what I have, and by God's grace, I walked into that bathroom a nervous wreck, afraid I would soon be on the local late-night news, but walked out so calm and relaxed. It really made a world of difference just to take a moment and turn to the Lord for peace, because He honestly granted me the greatest peace! Nothing about my circumstances had changed except my perspective. I had lost focus on God and had begun to focus on the world and all the problems that come with it; but when I took a sincere moment to seek Him, He found me, and no words can come close to describing the peace I found. —Rebekah S.

You may very well have had the experience of pouring out your heart to God in prayer and not being able to tell what His answer was, or even if He was saying anything to you at all. True, He may not give you His answer or solution at the exact time you hoped for it. But He will always respond at the right and the best time.

What a privilege to be able to pour out your emotions before the God of the universe and not be condemned as a result, but instead to be loved and taught! And that is how you will be received, my friend, when you come to Jesus. You will be loved and instructed. Remember that He is gentle and lowly in heart. He's not harsh with you. Yes, if you need correction, He will absolutely give it, not in a harsh or demeaning way, but in a loving way.

• •

Jen N. recalls a time when she was up all night with her three-year-old. The family was participating in a mission trip, and the church in which they were staying was very cold. Jen's daughter fussed and cried in discomfort for hours. Without Jesus, Jen is sure she wouldn't have made it through that night. "I just prayed and gave [my daughter] to God," Jen says. "It kept me calm; it made her calmer. Just knowing that you have prayer can keep you from reaching a breaking point."

• •

Resting Mentally in Jesus

For me, this one is sometimes the most difficult of all.

I'm a thinker. I enjoy pastimes, hobbies and pursuits where you have to think. I even enjoy studying Greek grammar (I'm a teaching assistant for a biblical Greek class). Granted, I also very much enjoy simple leisure pursuits (in fact, I'm writing this chapter before my husband and I—and Timmy—attend a Major League Baseball game tonight). But I like to think.

There's nothing wrong with thinking. The problem comes when you rely too much on your own thinking to determine your emotions or to find answers.

Jesus knows far, far more than I do. His ways are not my ways, and His thoughts are not my thoughts (see Isa. 55:8). Yet, too often,

I rely on my own thought processes to work out the solution to a problem. I turn a situation around and around in my head, trying to look at it from every angle and figure out what I'm going to do.

Of course, this kind of thinking does not lead to mental rest. It leads to anxiety, worry and tension.

Perhaps you know the feeling. Maybe you also tend to try to work things out on your own and have a difficult time being at peace when there's a situation to be dealt with or a problem to be solved. If that's the case, resting mentally in Jesus probably sounds like a pretty great idea to you, as it does to me, if only you could figure out how to let go and do it.

Actually, it's simple. It's not easy, but it's simple. Resting mentally in Jesus involves affirming with our minds that Jesus is in control of everything that concerns us—of the whole world, actually. It involves continuing to stay tuned to Jesus' voice so that we can hear Him when He speaks. Finally, it means refusing to become anxious or worried and instead making a deliberate effort to rest mentally in Jesus each time we are tempted to let our mind start going around in circles.

For example, let's say you are confronting a particular behavior problem with your child. Let's say your child argues with you when you give him an answer he doesn't like. You could choose to turn this problem around and around in your mind, looking at it from every which way, getting more and more frustrated and angry in the process because you can't come up with a solution that will work. Or, you could choose to turn the problem over to Jesus, saying something like, "Jesus, this is too big for me. I don't know what to do in order to train my child the way I should. Will you help me?" Then, each time the problem comes into your mind, you take it before Jesus. Tell Him you know He's already got an answer planned, even though you can't see it. Tell Him you know He can handle it even though you can't, and you're going to leave it at His feet for Him to carry.

Or maybe the behavior problem is yours. Maybe you've struggled with anger, impatience or some other trait that is harmful to your family. Do the same thing: Instead of becoming more and more frustrated in trying to get rid of your sin, turn the problem over to Jesus.

• •

Anger. Every single day of my life I struggle with anger.
I get angry when I have to tell the kids 27 times to come to dinner. I get angry when my husband points out that I'm getting angry. I get angry when I'm driving behind a bread truck going too slow. I get angry when the neighbor's dog barks incessantly. I have been working at this raw emotion of mine for a while now. I've been asking God to give me peace when I can feel it start bubbling up from within. I don't want to be remembered as a mother who is constantly screaming like a crazy person. I want my kids to see Christ in my everyday dealings with them, and every day I feel like I've failed. I know that God provides the grace to forgive my mistakes. I know that He provides new mercies every day. I need to continue to ask for God's help daily and learn from my frequent screw-ups. I need to quit trying to attain perfection and focus more on the improvements I've made. I am so grateful that we serve a God who is so quick to forgive our shortcomings and so gracious to give us new strength in every moment of every day. —Trish C.

• •

This doesn't mean you won't ever think about the issue again; of course you will. But it does mean that when you do think about it, you and Jesus will think about it together. You will let Jesus carry the burden of trying to figure out what to do. You will remain attentive to Jesus' voice, and you will keep seeking Him and His answer, but you won't try to force your mind to come up with something on its own. You will let Him be in control.

It's an incredible privilege that Jesus even allows us to rest in Him. Why would we not do it?

After all, when we rest physically in Him, we get His strength added to our own, and we may even get more physical rest. When we rest spiritually in Him, we get peace for our souls. When we rest emotionally in Him, we get peace in our emotions, and when we rest mentally in Him, we get—yep, you guessed it—peace in our minds.

Jesus has got us covered—body, spirit, heart and mind—if we will just let Him do the job He wants to do.

Rest in Him, dear mom. Let Him refresh you.

Going Deeper

Do you get the physical, spiritual, emotional and mental rest you need? If not, ask Jesus to refresh you. Ask Him to show you where, when and how to get the rest He wants you to have.

_____

_____

_____

_____

_____

_____

_____

_____

_____

_____

_____

_____

_____

_____

_____

_____

_____

_____

Delighting in Jesus

For more than seven years, my daughter Ellie was the biggest Hello Kitty fan you ever saw. She had a Hello Kitty comforter set and Hello Kitty sheets. She had stuffed Hello Kitties and knick-knack Hello Kitties. She had clothes with her hero's face on them; she had a Hello Kitty umbrella; and she had Hello Kitty posters. Not to mention all the Hello Kitty toys, eating utensils and school supplies.

Whenever we were in a store somewhere to buy Ellie something she needed, she would always look for one with Hello Kitty on it. When we passed something that was Hello Kitty (a water cooler, a toaster, even a microwave), she'd say, "Look! Hello Kitty!"

I can remember countless times when she'd hug something with Hello Kitty on it and bury her face in it, grinning hugely.

In other words, she loved Hello Kitty. Better yet, she delighted in Hello Kitty.

If you have a child who is in love with something—dinosaurs or Dora, soccer balls or stuffed animals—you know what true delight looks like on your child's face. You've probably even bought some favored item on impulse just so you could delight your child's heart. You love seeing your child revel in something he or she loves.

That's the kind of delight we can have in Jesus. Not just the kind of delight we're *supposed* to have, but the kind it's actually possible to have.

We know we're supposed to love Jesus. We get that. But delight in Him? Most of us don't understand what that would look like. Does it mean we go to church every time the doors are open? Does it mean we raise our hands when we sing? Maybe we should spend 30 minutes every day praying?

All of those things are good, but none of those things is what it means to delight in Jesus. If you want to go to church frequently, fine. If you want to raise your hands when you sing (or if you don't), fine. If you spend time every day praying, of course that's fine. But these are all actions. Good actions, to be sure, but actions nonetheless. And while delighting in Jesus will naturally result in some actions, it's primarily a matter of the heart.

• •

I'm all "Ms. OCD Perfectionist" when it comes to my cakes, and I am certainly my worst critic. But when Alex made his own birthday cake this year, it was very simple and plain. [It was] a three-tiered cake frosted white, which he tried to frost but ended up with more of a "crumb coat" each time, to which he added candy clay Batman 2 figures that he made himself. To me, Ms. OCD Perfectionist, I saw a plain, drab, needed-something-more cake. But to my not-quite-eight-year-old son, it was awesomeness. He had made his own cake, and the figures, and he was so proud of himself. He had the biggest smile on his face, and I had to catch myself and wipe away the look of disappointment that I know had to be obvious. I smiled as big as I could and asked if he was proud of himself, and he nodded yes. It made me think, *Something so simple and yet he's so happy about it!* I couldn't have done a better job myself. Simplicity . . . how wonderful the world would be if we could all have the eyes and the heart of a child! —Rebekah S.

• •

Ellie could have requested Hello Kitty on all her clothes even if she didn't care that much about Hello Kitty, because she thought it was what she was supposed to do. She could have asked for Hello Kitty pencils and notebooks for school because she thought it would please me, even though it didn't really matter to her. In other words, she could have done the same actions she did but for far different reasons.

We all know what it's like to perform religious actions out of a sense of obligation or duty. We've all had times when we went to church, prayed or read our Bible even when our heart wasn't really in it. But we did it because we thought we were supposed to.

That's not delighting in Jesus.

True, even when we don't feel warm, fuzzy feelings about reading the Bible, we should still do it on a regular basis. We shouldn't depend on feelings to be our motivation for praying or for attending church. Sometimes those feelings will be there, and sometimes they won't. If we only do the right thing when we *feel* like it, we'll be absurdly inconsistent. So doing the right thing even when it doesn't give you warm fuzzies is good, but it's not delighting in Jesus.

Granted, you won't always have warm, fuzzy feelings for spending time with Jesus either. But if we went through life constantly feeling intense feelings, can you imagine how exhausted we would be? Not always feeling a certain way doesn't necessarily mean anything. (It might mean something if you *never* feel delight, but it's not automatic. Sometimes God asks us to walk through a time when we don't have those exciting feelings. He knows they'll come back. He wants to give us the opportunity to remain close to Him even when our feelings aren't impelling us to do so.)

So if delighting in Jesus doesn't mean we'll always have warm fuzzies, what *does* it mean?

Delighting in Jesus is when your heart—not just your head—desires Him. It's when you want to be with Him. It's when what makes you happy is being with Him. It's when you miss Him if you're apart for too long.

In this chapter, we'll explore how that works and how it can make a difference in the life of a mom.

Desiring Him with Your Heart

My daughter Lindsey has two best friends. Both of these little girls are great kids, and Lindsey has tons of fun whenever she is with either of them. How did they get to be best friends? By spending time together, getting to know each other and finding in each other a kindred spirit.

• •

On February 24, 2009, I fell and broke my right kneecap. I had surgery to repair the kneecap, and following the surgery, I went through several weeks of very painful therapy. I had always thought of myself as being pretty strong emotionally, and pretty self-sufficient. In other words, I liked being the one doing and not so much the one receiving . . . especially where the pain was involved. But suddenly, I found myself on the receiving end, depending on friends and family to do things for me and help me in ways that I never would have chosen. Also, during this time, little by little, and without my realizing what was happening, I slipped into depression and anxiety. My doctor had me try several different kinds of anti-depressants, but my sensitivity to medication prevented me from being able to take the medication. I finally sought the help of a Christian counselor. She was great, but she was limited in what she could do. I am thankful that Jesus was there for me then, that He is with me now, and that He will be with me in the future. Through it all, I have learned and am learning to delight in Jesus. We do not usually view accidents, or any bad things, as blessings, but I know that God has used and is using this for my good and His glory. —Elna B.

• •

That's exactly how it develops between us and Jesus. In order to come to love Him, we have to spend time with Him. It's hard to love someone you don't really know. When we spend time with Jesus, we come to know Him. And when we come to know Him as He truly is, we will also love Him.

As the song says, "To know, know, know Him is to love, love, love Him." It sounds like a cliché, but it's true. It's simply not possible to know Jesus as He truly is without loving Him.

In fact, I'll take it a step further: To the extent that you don't love Jesus, you don't truly know Him.

How can I make a statement like that? Because Jesus is completely lovable. It's not possible to truly know such a wonderful, lovable person and have any reaction other than loving Him back. To suggest otherwise is to say that Jesus, even when people truly know Him, is incapable of inspiring love in some of them because He's just not lovable enough. It's to say that Jesus is not always worthy of love.

There are many wonderful ways to get to know Jesus: You can attend a church where the Bible is taught; participate in a small group of friends who want to learn to love Jesus more too; pray and study your Bible on your own; listen to Christian music and/or praise and worship music; attend retreats and conferences; memorize portions of Scripture; or take time just to be with Jesus, with no particular agenda in mind except to follow His leading for your time together.

Oh, and one more thing: Come before Him with a sincere heart, asking Him to help you know Him better. That's another request you can be sure to receive a yes to, because it's completely in line with His will. Of course, your heart must be sincere, because you can't put anything over on Jesus, and He is probably not going to reveal Himself to someone who isn't interested in Him.

Even if you're not really interested in building a relationship with Him, but you know you should be, take that before Him too. Ask Him to increase your desire for Him (which is a great request no matter where you are in your spiritual journey). Tell Him you want to love Him more than you do. Be honest. After all, He already knows the truth. Being honest before Him is one way of showing Him that you are sincere and that you care about being with Him.

So That Your Children Will Know Him

The second reason it's important for you to know Jesus—besides the fact that it will make every difference in your life—is that if you don't know Jesus very well, your children will have a harder time coming to know Him. Likewise, if you know Him well, your children will be more likely to know Him accurately.

Why is this? For one thing, children learn by example more than they learn by instruction. You've heard the phrase "Do as I say, not as I do"? Ridiculous when it comes to rearing kids. Most kids will do what you do, regardless of what you say. Even the ones who somehow do the right thing despite your actions will have a harder time of it if you're not providing a good example for them to follow.

If your kids see you making a relationship with Jesus a priority for yourself and your family, they are much more likely to desire a relationship with Him. How can you do that? Let's talk about several ways.

Let Your Kids See You Spending Time with Jesus

I remember one morning about a year ago when I woke up early. I actually woke up on my own, feeling fairly rested, before anybody else in the house was awake. *This would be a great time to spend some time with Jesus*, I thought. I gathered my Bible and prayer book and sat down in my favorite recliner for a little one-on-one time with my Savior.

I had no sooner opened my Bible and turned a page when I heard a bedroom door open at the other end of the house. A few seconds later, the door closed, and little footsteps started making their way toward me. I closed my Bible and sighed. I don't know how they do it, but my kids seem to have some kind of inner radar for whenever I'm trying to get alone with Jesus. Somehow they know—and they always need something right then.

One option is to do what I did that day and give up on my quiet time. Another—and better—option would have been to let my child arrive in the room and see me reading my Bible. If he or she interrupted, I could have said, "Just a minute, sweetheart. Mommy's reading her Bible. Would you like to hear what God is saying?" I could then have read the passage to my child.

In which way would my child have learned more? Seeing me give up my quiet time or watching me put Jesus first? There may indeed be some times when your child's need requires that you put the Bible down. You should never say, "I'm sorry, but I can't minister to your legitimately urgent need; I'm talking to Jesus." One of the things Jesus has put you on this earth for is to help your children with their needs. But when the need isn't truly urgent and nobody will be harmed by having to wait a few minutes, let your child see you putting your time with God first.

You won't be making your child feel bad. You'll be making him or her feel secure.

Let Your Children Hear You Praying

I still remember Ellie's first prayer, which came when she was about 14 months old. She was sitting in her high chair, and I put her food in front of her. Ellie clasped her little hands, bowed her head and said, "Myna, myna, myna, myna. Amen." I don't know what she said, but I'll bet God knew.

Eventually, your children will have to move on from "myna myna." What better way to teach them how to do that than to show them an example of how to pray?

Jesus' disciples once asked Him to teach them to pray. They had observed His prayer life and they wanted to learn to pray like He did. That's exactly the reaction you want from your kids. You want them to see you praying and have the desire to pray like you. Not because they'll see the perfection of your prayers (if there even is such a thing), but because they'll see your heart for Jesus and want to know how to talk to Him like that.

Let's look at what happened when the disciples asked Jesus to teach them to pray.

Now Jesus was praying in a certain place, and when he finished, one of his disciples said to him, "Lord, teach us to pray, as John taught his disciples." And he said to them, "When you pray, say: Our Father which art in heaven, Hallowed be thy name. Thy kingdom come. Thy will be done in earth, as it is in heaven. Give us this day our daily bread.

And forgive us our debts, as we forgive our debtors. And lead us not into temptation, but deliver us from evil: For thine is the kingdom, and the power, and the glory, for ever. Amen. " (See Luke 11:1-2; cf. Matt. 6:9-13.)

Notice what Jesus did *not* say. He didn't say, "Here, read these scrolls and get back to Me." Nor did He launch into an extended explanation. He simply provided His disciples an example.

Having your children read about prayer or giving them a verbal explanation is fine. But you also need to give them an example. You can tell them all day long that prayer is fun, and you can talk about how much you love Jesus. But if your children *see* you loving Jesus and talking to Him, they'll really get it. And that's what you want.

Let Your Children See You Happily Come Under Jesus' Authority

Recently, while driving our minivan with my five children inside, I saw red and blue flashing lights behind me. I immediately began to pull over even though I didn't know why I was being stopped. I assumed that it was for speeding and that I hadn't been watching my speedometer closely enough.

As I waited for the officer to approach my car, I calmly explained to the kids that a police officer was telling Mommy to stop, and I had obeyed, because God has placed police officers as a legitimate authority over our lives. I explained that if we don't do anything wrong, we have no need to be afraid. Police officers are there to help punish those who do wrong (see 1 Pet. 2:13-14), and apparently I had done something wrong. I was therefore obeying the officer's instructions to stop and find out what I had done.

It turned out that I had misunderstood a directional sign posted in a construction area. (This was the first time I had driven through the area while it was under construction.) Fortunately, the officer was gracious and let me go with only a warning. But, as I told the kids on the way home, if he had issued me a ticket, I would have had to pay it, because I must obey God-ordained authority.

How different the experience would have been for my kids if I had ranted and raved about the officer's actions (even if he couldn't hear me at the time), about how I didn't deserve a ticket and maybe even about how he should be out catching the "real" offenders (when I was a 911 dispatcher, I heard this statement many times). Instead, as it was, they learned that Mommy is willing to come under God's authority with a good attitude even when I'd rather not have to.

I'm pretty sure that experience and the way I handled it taught them a lot more than any lectures on my part would have. Maybe the next time they have to come under my authority when they don't want to, they will remember this incident and how Mommy came under authority. Perhaps I'll even remind them about it.

Let Your Children See You Living Your Talk

Perhaps one of the greatest things a mom can do for her children—one of the biggest ways that what she does matters—is to let them see you living the way Jesus says to live. In other words, live before them in integrity.

It's easy to tell our children to be honest and kind and to work hard. It's much harder to actually do those things, especially when we're tempted to do exactly the opposite.

If you tell your children to be honest, but then you ask them to tell an unwanted telephone caller you're not home when you really are, what will they learn?

If you tell them to be kind but then you verbally tear people down behind their backs, what will your children learn?

If you tell them to work hard but they see you sitting on the couch all day watching TV, what message do you think they'll get?

For me, the biggest challenge in the area of living my talk comes in the twin areas of being patient and speaking kindly. Usually, those two go hand in hand—when I feel impatient with someone, I sometimes don't speak kindly. I may speak snappishly or even with disgust. Yet I require my children to speak kindly to their siblings, and I even discipline them when they don't. Perhaps you can think of an area where you require your children to do the right thing but have difficulty doing the right thing yourself.

. . . .

Tonya G. remembers the time when she took some homemade bread to a stranger she sees nearly every time she passes by his home. She and her children had been discussing being the hands and feet for Jesus as well as the fact that once we ask Him to come into our hearts, He does come in, and if He asks us to do something (she felt He had told her to bake this man some bread), we are to do what He has commanded.

. . . .

Granted, we will never be perfect, and children understand that. They won't conclude that there's a disconnect between our walk and our talk if we only sin in a certain way occasionally—especially if we apologize (we'll look at that in the next section). But if a certain sin becomes a habit, our children will know it. They'll also wonder why they have to obey but we don't. They'll conclude that mommy really doesn't mean what she says and that living Jesus' way really isn't important after all.

What you do in this area matters immensely, moms. Do you want your children to think that living Jesus' way is right, good and satisfying? Then show them that it is by doing it.

Apologize to Your Children When You Have Sinned Against Them

Perhaps, like I did, you grew up in a home where your parents never (or almost never) initiated an apology to you for sinning against you. Perhaps you simply can't imagine why you should ever need to apologize to your children; after all, you're the mom!

In this section, we're going to look at how vitally important it is that you be willing to apologize when you have sinned. We'll look at what it teaches your children when you are willing to apologize, and what they learn when you're not.

I still cringe when I remember an incident when Ellie was about 18 months old. I was having a bad day, and I was mad about something that had nothing to do with her. I stomped into her room to put some clean clothes in her dresser. Ellie followed me in. "Mommy?" she asked.

I turned to her and yelled, "What!" It wasn't even a question, really. Immediately, Ellie burst into tears. I felt awful.

I knelt down in front of Ellie and drew her into my arms, holding her tight. "Mommy's so sorry, Ellie," I told her over and over. "Mommy shouldn't have yelled. You didn't do anything wrong. I'm sorry."

I wish I could say that's the only incident where I ever had to apologize to one of my children, but I can't. There have been other times. You've had those times too—times when you do something or fail to do something and realize (maybe right away, maybe later) that you blew it. You messed up, and your child didn't deserve your response.

• •

Recently, my grown daughter and I were putting up groceries together. As we chatted, suddenly our conversation took a surprising twist and Leslie snapped at me and then left the room.

A few minutes later, I felt arms slip around my waist. "Mom . . . can I have a do-over?" Leslie asked, tears in her eyes. "That wasn't your fault. I'm just so tired."

She was a new mom and exhausted. Her baby was far from sleeping through the night.

As I pulled my beautiful daughter close, time slipped backwards to when I was a young mom to three under the age of two. There were so many times that I was overwhelmed or sleep deprived, and though I loved motherhood, I felt as if I fell short often.

As our kids grew up, we created a family tradition. It was the "do-over." If mom or dad or one of the kids said or did something they wished they hadn't, each was allowed one do-over per day.

A do-over meant that we were sorry. It meant that we would offer a sincere apology, or try to make it right if we could.

But it also meant that the slate was wiped clean. Our mistake wouldn't come back to haunt us in a conversation or at another time. We didn't need do-overs every day, but when we did, it was a beautiful way to start fresh.

As I held my daughter, I treasured the fact that this family tradition—the ability to apologize and start over—was moving into the next generation.

After all, every one needs a do-over once in a while.

—T. Suzanne Eller, author

• •

What do you do then? Do you figure, *Ah, well, she'll probably forget all about it*? Do you justify yourself and blame your child, saying, *Well, she made me mad!*? Or do you go to your child, get down on your child's level and apologize sincerely and humbly from your heart?

Around our house, we have a way to apologize. The offender must say, "I'm sorry for" and specifically name the sin. Not, "I'm sorry for being mean," but "I'm sorry for snapping at you." Then the offender says, "I should have (fill in the blank)," and names specifically what he or she should have done in that situation (not just, "I should have been nice," but "I should have spoken to you kindly"). Then the offender says, "Will you forgive me?"

It's humbling to have to ask for forgiveness, but it's oh-so-necessary. Why? Because your child's heart needs to hear you ask. Because the relationship between you and your child needs to be put right, and you, as the mom and the offender, should initiate it. And also because when you demonstrate sincere repentance from your sins, you teach your children how to admit their sins, repent and seek forgiveness.

All of us know someone who never admits to being wrong. Whatever this person does that offends somebody is never a legitimate sin—it's either the offended person's fault for being too sensitive or the offender's being misunderstood or some other excuse. In order for your children to stay close to Jesus in a growing, loving relationship—not to mention stay close to others—they will have to know how to acknowledge sin.

What kind of marriage do you think your children will have if they don't know how to acknowledge wrongdoing? What kind of parent or employee will they be? The answer is obvious. If they don't know how to acknowledge sin, they will go through life leaving a trail of broken people in their wake and feeling bewildered about why everyone "misunderstands" them. That's not what I want for my children, and I know it's not what you want for yours.

But acknowledging sin is only the first step. Your children need to know how to repent. They need to see what it looks like to be sorry for sin and acknowledge what they should have done instead. Many people today know that they do things that society or the Bible considers wrong behavior, but they don't care. It simply doesn't matter to them. These people are going to have an extremely hard time forming healthy relationships with healthy people, because no one wants to be in a close relationship with someone who is never sorry for what they do wrong. Your children need to see you swallowing your pride and putting the restoration of a relationship first rather than trying to maintain a perfect image. When you do this on a consistent basis, your children will know how to do it too.

Finally, your children need to learn how to ask forgiveness and move on. Let's say they've admitted their sin and repented. They know what they did, and they're sorry for it. Being sorry does little good if they're not willing to make things right with the offended party. In fact, the Bible clearly illustrates this principle:

> So if you are offering your gift at the altar and there remember that your brother has something against you, leave your gift there before the altar and go. First be reconciled to your brother, and then come and offer your gift (Matt. 5:23-24).

In other words, make things right. Approach the other person and ask for his or her forgiveness. Show that you care that you've hurt or offended them.

Then, once you've done that, move on.

We all know people who can't get over some sin they've committed in their past. They continue to torment themselves with their guilt even though they've acknowledged it, repented of it and sought forgiveness. They may even say things like, "I know Jesus forgives me, but I just can't forgive myself."

Do you want your children to get bogged down in their guilt and never be able to move on, even when they've done everything the Bible says to do (admit, repent and ask forgiveness)? Of course you don't. And if you don't, you will have to show your children how to move on.

You don't move on in such a way that you forget all about what you've done and do the same thing again. You don't move on as if what you did didn't really matter all that much. You move on knowing what you did, but also knowing, believing and living out that you are forgiven. You do not allow any temptations to believe otherwise to keep your emotions bound to your past sin. If you remember your sin again, you use it as an occasion to praise Jesus for forgiving you, not to remind yourself how bad you should feel. Jesus has set you free. You need to teach your children that when Jesus says you are free, He means it. Show them by living it out that if the Son sets you free, you are free indeed (see John 8:36). Teach them to delight in the wonderful character of Jesus that causes Him to grant you such amazing forgiveness.

Mom, if you delight in Jesus and live it out in such a way that your delight spills over to your children, they will benefit from the abundance of your and Jesus' relationship, and you will have given them the best gift you can possibly give. Not only that, but when you are delighting in Jesus and obeying His commands, every other area of your life will fall into place.

Going Deeper

Do you delight in Jesus? Do your kids see you delighting in Him? If not, confess this to Him. Ask Him to help you know Him better so that you will delight in Him.

Serving in Jesus

When you're asked to think about someone who is truly a servant of Jesus, who comes to mind?

For me, it's Billy Graham.

Billy Graham has been preaching the good news of Jesus for 70 years. Seventy years! And he hasn't done it halfheartedly. He's traveled the world, as well as the United States, holding crusades and pouring out every effort to make sure that everybody everywhere in the world has heard about Jesus.

It's not like he only preaches out of obligation, either. If you've ever heard Billy preach, whether on TV or in person, it's obvious that he really loves Jesus. It's equally obvious that he and Jesus have a close relationship. Billy doesn't claim to be perfect. He acknowledges that he is a sinner just like every other human being. But the fact that he loves Jesus shines through in everything he says and does—even every expression on his face and every gesture.

Billy Graham is a servant of Jesus.

But does he have a greater ministry than you or I do as moms? No.

No? How can I say that when Billy Graham has preached to millions of people and brought millions of them to Christ?

Simply this: The greatness of a ministry doesn't consist in the number of people reached. The greatness of a ministry is found in the greatness of the one who calls you to that ministry.

Billy Graham has a great ministry not because of the numbers of people he has reached, but because Jesus, who called him, is great. Jesus had a task He wanted done, and He assigned it to Billy. Billy obeyed fully and willingly, and millions of people were saved. Jesus is pleased with Billy, but not merely because of the numbers of people saved. Billy didn't save those people; Jesus did. What Jesus is pleased with is Billy's heart.

Likewise, Jesus has called you to a particular ministry. He had a task to be done, and He assigned it to you. If you obey Him with a willing heart, He will be equally pleased with you as He is with Billy Graham. And your ministry will be just as great, because the same Jesus who called Billy has called you—and remember that the greatness of ministry depends on the one who calls, not on what the world would term "greatness."

So you have been called to a great ministry. All moms have. But most of us don't realize this fact. It's kind of like waiting to board an airplane. There's one line for the VIP travelers and one line for the rest of us. If you're a VIP (according to the airline), you get special treatment. You get to board first. You probably get other stuff too, though I wouldn't know, because I'm not an airline VIP. The point is, most of us assume we're not VIPs in terms of what we contribute in life. We think moms merely stand with the rest of the non-VIP crowd, probably somewhere in the back. We'll get to board later, once the people who really matter have had their chance.

Nothing could be further from the truth.

In terms of Christ's calling, there is no difference between those who respond. It's not that some of us are VIPs and the rest of us—the great majority of us—are merely part of the common herd.

As far as Christ is concerned, all of us are VIPs. Let's look at that subject from a passage in the book of James:

> For if a man wearing a gold ring and fine clothing comes into your assembly, and a poor man in shabby clothing also comes in, and if you pay attention to the one who wears the fine clothing and say, "You sit here in a good place," while you say to the poor man, "You stand over there," or, "Sit down at my feet," have you not then made distinctions among yourselves and become judges with evil thoughts? (Jas. 2:2-4).

Most of us have read this passage before, but we usually don't look at it deeply enough. We know that Jesus is saying not to prefer one person over another just because of clothes and money, but we don't usually stop to think about *why* He is saying this.

Jesus wants all people, no matter their circumstances, to be treated equally, because circumstances don't matter to Him. In fact, He is the one who has designed or allowed those circumstances. So He's not impressed with someone's wealth, because it really came from Him anyway. He knows that circumstances aren't what matter. What matters is that every person is a human being, and therefore, in the sense of how they should be treated, on equal footing.

Likewise, Jesus doesn't prefer someone over you because of what the world would term a "greater" calling. He is the one who assigned callings anyway. He's not going to give you a seemingly more modest calling and then think you're not important because the world would see what He gave you as insignificant. He is well aware that your calling is significant because of Him, not because of how it looks to the world.

• •

Amanda L. knows that her job as a mom "is important, is worthy, is the most important job out there. But at the same time, it's one of the most mundane, unappreciated jobs. It's a daily struggle for me to keep all of that in perspective."

• •

You, in your calling, are just as valuable to Jesus as someone who preaches to millions. You, as a mom, are just as important to Him as someone whose name is a household word because of his or her contributions to society.

That's because while the world looks at external factors, Jesus looks at your heart (see 1 Sam. 16:7). *That's* what determines your usefulness to God's kingdom—the state of your heart, not the nature of your calling.

Besides, did you realize that you have opportunities to personally serve Jesus in ways that even people like Billy Graham don't have?

Physically Caring for Jesus

Remember the poem from chapter 6 called "Loving Jesus"? It illustrated how everything we do for our children, we are doing directly for Jesus. In other words, when we feed, clothe and bathe our children, we are feeding, clothing and bathing Jesus.

Young children are in desperate need of having someone do for them, or help them do, all the tasks necessary to take physical care of their bodies. As they grow, they become more able to help themselves, but they don't start out that way. Babies are completely unable to take care of themselves. The only thing they can do is cry to let you know they need something. They can't feed themselves, bathe themselves, change their diapers or clothe themselves. Left to their own devices, they would lie in the same place for months until they developed mobility, if they ever did.

So when you take care of your baby, you are taking care of Jesus in an intimate, practical way. Remember that Jesus was once a tiny baby in need of all the same help your baby needs. He couldn't feed, clothe or bathe Himself. He even needed His diapers changed. So when you minister to your baby, you are ministering to Jesus just as surely as His mother Mary once ministered to Him.

Emotionally Caring for Jesus

Lindsey walked slowly toward me, her head bent, tears pooling in her eyes and running down her cheeks. "Mommy, I'm sad about Pumpkin," she said.

Pumpkin was our cat who had died the day before. Lindsey had really loved him, so of course she was grieving.

What do you think I did in response? Do you think I told her, "Well, tough, he's just an animal. Get over it"? Of course not! That would have been complete disregard for and invalidation of my daughter's emotions. It would have been ignoring her need for emotional care at that moment. Had I merely provided clothes and meals for her that day, I wouldn't have done enough.

I held out my arms to Lindsey, and she crawled up on the couch and snuggled next to me. I held her as she cried, and I stroked her hair.

In those moments, I was caring for Jesus and His emotions. I was showing Him that I not only cared about one of His precious lambs, but that I cared for Him.

True, Jesus doesn't have the same kind of emotions we humans do. His emotions are always perfectly justified, righteous and holy, whereas ours . . . well, aren't. But Jesus identifies so strongly with Lindsey—and with my other children, and with yours—that when I cared for her, I was caring for Him.

I'm sure that when Jesus was a little boy on this earth, there were times when He was sad. Maybe He scraped His knee, or maybe a beloved pet died. When He went running to Mary for comfort, do you think she said, "You're the Son of God; get over it"? Hardly. She wouldn't have said that any more than you or I would tell our child to get over it. So now, when we comfort our children, He receives further comfort from us.

Helping our kids have fun is also caring for them emotionally. It shows them that their emotions of joy and excitement are important to us. It shows them that we care that they get to feel these fun emotions. It shows Jesus that we care about making Him happy too.

My daughter often befriended new students in school. She would help them in whatever way they needed help. On a few occasions, when the new student became acquainted with other students and knew her way around, she would no longer have anything to do with my daughter. This would be hurtful to my daughter. In the same way I comforted my son, I tried to comfort my daughter. I would hug her, talk to her and try to comfort her with hugs and words. I remember saying to her that I knew God was pleased that she was helping these new students, and I told her how proud I was of her for doing so. —Elna B.

Spiritually Caring for Jesus

Jesus wasn't born knowing everything about the Scriptures. Does that surprise you? But the Bible shows several instances of His learning (for instance, take that time when Jesus' parents realized somebody had left Him behind, and they found Him in the temple). Jesus needed to be taught.

Granted, He never said, "We're studying the Torah *again?*" or "Why do I have to learn this stuff?" Teaching Him was probably a pleasure, all the time, especially since His understanding would have been unclouded by sin, and He would have been able to learn things in a way that we sinful human beings cannot.

Even so, Jesus needed to be taught. He needed His parents to spend time with Him, telling Him the stories handed down from previous generations, teaching Him portions of Scripture, patiently explaining it to Him, answering His questions and taking Him to synagogue. Jesus needed to hear His parents talking about God the Father; He needed to see them living as God commands us to live; and He needed their encouragement when doing the right thing was hard (not that He ever sinned, but I'm sure He benefited from their spiritual encouragement anyway).

When you read your kids Bible stories or explain why you and your family don't participate in a certain activity, you are showing Jesus that you care about His spiritual knowledge as well. Not that Jesus needs to be taught by us; far from it. But again, He loves little children so much and identifies with them so strongly that when we minister to our children's spiritual needs, Jesus says we have ministered to Him as well.

Mentally Caring for Jesus

Have you ever tried to explain something to your child, delivered what you felt was an excellent, patient, thorough explanation, and had your child look up at you and say, with a confused look on his or her face, "Huh?"

There were probably times when Jesus' parents tried to teach Him things and He simply didn't understand. Perhaps He needed Joseph to explain more than once how you form a table leg out of a raw piece of wood. Maybe He needed Mary to tell Him several times the directions on how to walk to a friend's house.

Your kids—and mine—will likewise need to be taught many things. They may even need to be taught repeatedly until they grasp the concept. I used to think (before I had kids) that when I wanted my children to do something, all I would have to do would be to explain what I wanted, and then the issue would be solved. Forever. There would never be any misunderstandings or confusion. They would never forget what I said. I would never hear, "How do you do that again?"

• •

I have learned that I hate to repeat myself. It finally dawned on me that this was pride. I thought what I had to say was so important that it should be heard, understood, appreciated and maybe even rejoiced in the first time I said it. The Lord showed me that He Himself does not treat me this way. He is kind and patient and shows me things as I'm ready. I now desire to teach my children the way the Holy Spirit teaches me—with patience, kindness and much grace. I don't always succeed, but even with the failures, I get to apologize and see my children forgive with grace. God is good! —Angela H.

• •

Yeah, I know. It doesn't work that way. Kids need repeats and re-do's. (So do adults, for that matter.) They need patient explanations and step-by-step instructions. Sometimes they need to be walked through a process before they can master it on their own.

It can be frustrating. Believe me, I've been there, and I'm sure you have too. But let's always remember that when we patiently train our children, we are training Jesus. Not because we have any knowledge He doesn't have, but because He has chosen to identify with our children. He says that whatever we do for them, we do for Him.

Why Does Jesus Call Women to Motherhood?

Have you ever thought about the answer to this question? *Why* exactly does Jesus assign some women to motherhood?

The answer is beautiful and incredible, and it's simply this: Jesus desires the kind of personal service a mom can give. Yes, He wants us to take care of our children, but there's more to it than that. He wants to receive our personal service. Yours. Mine.

Jesus wants the kind of intimate, loving service that moms provide. Just think about that for a minute: Jesus called you to what you do because He wants to receive that kind of service from you. He wants you to minister to Him in that way.

Granted, I'm sure He has other purposes for calling us to be moms. Our being a mom probably figures into His grand scheme for the universe in ways we can't even imagine. But never think that a calling is an impersonal thing with Jesus. He doesn't call you to something He doesn't really care about. He calls you to your job as a mom because it's important to Him and because He wants personally to receive your ministry.

What kind of personal ministry are you offering Him? Is it willing, sacrificial and loving?

What you do matters, mom. You do it to and for Jesus.

Going Deeper

Did you realize that Jesus desires the kind of service that moms can provide, which some other people cannot? Thank Him for calling you to such an important role and giving you the privilege to serve Him in this way.

Seeing Like Jesus

Sometimes, reading Jesus' words makes me think, "Huh?"

There are many examples in Scripture where Jesus says something I don't expect Him to say, where He takes the conversation onto a completely different track, or where He does something entirely unforeseen.

Had I been in any of those situations, I would have spoken or acted much differently. Yet Jesus always did exactly the right thing, and He acted immediately, while I would still have been standing there scratching my head, trying to figure out how to approach the problem.

Jesus always saw the true nature of the problem. And that helped Him know exactly how to approach it.

It's a skill that we would do well to develop as moms—seeing the true nature of what is before us.

Can you imagine how much easier discipline would be if we always knew the exact nature of the dispute and the root causes? How much more effective could we be in ministering to our children if we could see into their hearts, all the way to the root need, which might be very different from the need they expressed?

Mom, how you and I deal with our kids, matters. It's significant, because our actions teach them about our family, our world and, most importantly, our God. So we would do very well to make sure we are seeing clearly—seeing like Jesus—when we mother.

• •

Much of the time, the "real need" is either some sort of validation of the child's sense of self or just plain old focused mommy attention. It can be very hard to calm down and recognize that need when they are clinging to your leg and screaming about something totally unrelated and/or unexpected. —Kirstie F.

• •

Discerning the Real Need

There's an interesting story in the Gospel of Mark:

> And when [Jesus] returned to Capernaum after some days, it was reported that he was at home. And many were gathered together, so that there was no more room, not even at the door. And he was preaching the word to them. And they came, bringing to him a paralytic carried by four men. And when they could not get near him because of the crowd, they removed the roof above him, and when they had made an opening, they let down the bed on which the paralytic lay. And when Jesus saw their faith, he said to the paralytic, "Son, your sins are forgiven" (Mark 2:1-5).

Jesus was getting pretty popular. People wanted to hear His teaching. But they *really* wanted to see His miracles, especially those where somebody got healed. So when the people of Capernaum found out Jesus was at home, they were excited. A bunch of people came to hear Jesus, and they crowded into the house. There wasn't even any more standing room left.

I imagine that the paralytic's friends had heard that Jesus was coming and gotten pretty excited. "Let's go!" they might have said. "Maybe Jesus will heal you!"

So they picked up the paralytic's mat and carried him to the house where Jesus was. The only problem was that when they got there, the place was packed. There was no way to get to Jesus through that kind of crowd. So they stood there outside and came up with a plan.

They climbed the outside stairs to the roof and began removing the roof right over where Jesus was standing. This may not have been as difficult as it sounds to us. Roofs in those days were flat. You had the support for the roof laid, and then you had thatch and probably other stuff covering it up. It wasn't like they were removing concrete. But they were desperate to have their friend healed, so they began tearing up some guy's roof.

I like to imagine the scene inside when chunks of straw began falling onto Jesus' listeners, and maybe even onto Jesus. People probably looked up and thought, *What in the world . . . ?* Then the hole got wider. And then, just to make the situation even crazier, some guy on a mat got lowered down right in front of Jesus.

This man's friends were desperate for him to be healed—desperate enough to start tearing up some homeowner's property. Desperate enough to interrupt the very Teacher from whom they were seeking help. Desperate enough to make a spectacle of themselves. And the paralytic was probably desperate too—desperate enough to allow himself to be put at the center of this display.

I'm sure it was obvious to everyone what the paralytic was hoping for. After all, you don't do all the things his friends did just because you can't find seats in a crowded room. You don't do all those things because you want to hear some teaching. You do them out of desperation. The man wanted to be healed, and everyone knew it.

What did Jesus say in response to all this? He said, "Your sins are forgiven."

This is where I go, "Huh?" Sins are forgiven? What about healing? That's what the poor guy really wanted. I bet the crowd was confused too.

But Jesus knew something they didn't know: He knew that having one's sins forgiven is even more important than having one's body healed. He saw the man's most basic need.

• •

"The love, respect, and confidence of my children was the sweetest reward I could receive for my efforts to be the woman I would have them copy" (Louisa May Alcott). I read this when I was a new mother, and it marked a turning point for me. Motherhood (and especially homeschooling) and the necessity of being that example for my children has given me spiritual clarity. To recognize that the ultimate goal of a Christian parent is to facilitate the salvation of her child's soul clears the way forward, not only in parenting but in one's own relationship with Christ. —Jennifer M.

• •

Likewise, we as moms need to discern the real need. When our child comes to us, head hanging low, and says she can't tie her shoes, we need to be aware that the real need isn't to have her shoes tied (though that's part of it). Her real need, as evidenced by her demeanor, is to feel confident and capable. If we merely tie her shoes without addressing her feelings, we've missed something.

When our son pesters his sister (not that this ever happens at our house . . . ahem), there could be any number of real needs. Maybe he needs to understand how to respect other people, especially females. Maybe he's tired or bored or lonely. Granted, he needs to stop pestering his sister. (In fact, around our house, we have a name for this: being a "pester-pants.") But if his root need is more sleep, and we deal with the situation as if he merely needs to know how to respect others, it's not going to be quite right. Or take it the other way around, and say he's had plenty of sleep and is in a great mood, but he just doesn't understand that girls often don't appreciate playing in the same way as boys. Telling him to take a nap is hardly going to help the situation.

It's important to know what's really going on. It's vital to see the real need. But how can we do this? We're not Jesus. We're not even close.

Fortunately, Jesus has made His wisdom available to us. In James 1:5, we read that if we lack wisdom, we should just ask, and it *will* be given to us. In other words, if we're not sure what the root cause is, we can ask. Then we can deal with the situation in the best way.

Discern Inner Attitudes

Remember how we said Jesus was getting to be a popular guy? Every now and then, even a Pharisee would invite Him for dinner. On one such occasion, Jesus was sitting at the table (which would have meant sitting on a cushion, kind of reclining on one hip while leaning against the table in front of Him, His legs and feet stretched out behind Him) when:

A woman of the city, who was a sinner, when she learned that he was reclining at table in the Pharisee's house, brought an alabaster flask of ointment, and standing behind him at his feet, weeping, she began to wet his feet with her tears and wiped them with the hair of her head and kissed his feet and anointed them with the ointment. Now when the Pharisee who had invited him saw this, he said to himself, "If this man were a prophet, he would have known who and what sort of woman this is who is touching him, for she is a sinner." And Jesus answering said to him, "Simon, I have something to say to you" (Luke 7:37-40).

Jesus was receiving the woman's worship, but all the Pharisee could see was that the woman was a prostitute. He therefore began thinking negative thoughts about Jesus and making assumptions about His character. Then the Scripture tells us, "And Jesus answering said . . ."

Did you catch that? *Answering*? Jesus hadn't been asked a question. The Pharisee was sitting there thinking His own self-righteous thoughts and hadn't said a word. Yet, Jesus *answered*.

In other words, Jesus knew the thoughts of the man's heart and responded to what hadn't even been spoken but what He knew was true.

Likewise, we as moms need to be able to correctly discern our children's attitudes in order to rebuke, encourage, correct or whatever is appropriate.

One caveat: We are not accurate mind readers like Jesus was. We run the very real risk of assuming we know what's in a person's heart but being wrong. Therefore, if we think we know the attitude of our child's heart is a negative one, we ought to double-check ourselves. If it's appropriate, we could talk to the child about it, asking questions and probing to try to discern what's really going on in that little head. An even more effective way is to ask Jesus if your impression of what is going on is correct. He'll tell you if it's not—if you're open to hearing Him, that is.

I have told my children that I pray and ask Jesus to help me know what is going on inside of them. I explain that I do this because I want to be the best mommy I can be, and in order to do that, I need Jesus' insight. I tell them I pray that Jesus will quickly make negative attitudes obvious so that I can help them correct those attitudes. But I also ask Jesus to make positive attitudes obvious as well so that I don't punish a child when it isn't deserved.

If our children know that we care about truly knowing them and making sure we are relating to them in the best possible way, it will make a huge difference in their lives. After all, think of how you would respond to a boss who flew off the handle any time he was angry and didn't bother to get the full details of the situation. You would probably get frustrated and discouraged. You might even get angry. Now magnify those feelings by a thousand, and you know how your children will feel when you don't take the time to deal rightly with them. Likewise, when you do take the time, there will be an equally positive response. Your children will know you care about them, and they'll respond with love for you. They'll be motivated to work harder and behave better than they would otherwise. And that's a winning situation for all concerned.

Give Them What They Need

I don't know about you, but Christmas always presents a challenge for me.

My husband and I set a budget each year for gifts for each child. Staying within the budget isn't the problem. The problem is maximizing those dollars. Since we don't have unlimited funds, that means we can only buy a certain number of gifts. So I always wind up spending a lot of time wondering which gift out of all the things they want would really please my children the most. Is a particular gift worth spending most of the budget on? Which gift will delight my child for about 10 minutes, then be forgotten and wind up getting donated somewhere because it never got played with? On the other hand, which gift would truly bring delight, not just on Christmas morning, but preferably for a long time afterward?

Discerning what to give my children for Christmas can be hard. I try to do the best I can. Some years I get it right, and some years, not so right.

As far as parenting, though, I want to get it "right" far more often than I get it "not right." I know that meeting my children's needs really matters. Meeting my kids' needs as a mom is about far more than what they open on Christmas morning. Meeting their needs on a regular basis—or failing to do so—is about shaping the kind of life my child will have. It's about helping my child become the kind of person Jesus made him or her to be.

I want to be sure I meet their true needs—not just what they think their needs are or what I think their needs are. I want to meet what Jesus says their needs are.

Sports activities? Educational toys? Play dates? All of these may be well and good, but they are not my child's most basic needs. Ultimately, Jesus says what my child really needs is to remain connected to Him and to others.

• •

The first year and a half after my daughter was born, I didn't have God in my life. I don't know how I made it. Now it's been seven years, and I talk to God all day, tell my daughter about God all the time, point out to her His work in my life, her life and our lives. I know He will be there for me no matter what. When I had my miscarriage this past January, I knew He was in control no matter what I thought. I just had to wait and see what would happen. I also told my daughter that God didn't do this to us; it was the devil and just living here on earth. I know that helped us get through, as well as knowing one day we will see our child again. —Jenny U.

• •

I talked in a previous chapter about how we can help our children stay connected to Jesus by constantly pointing them to Him, by demonstrating how lovely He is and by being an example of what being connected to Him looks like. We know this is important. Yet often we spend far more effort on other attempts to meet our children's needs than on meeting this most fundamental need. We spend more time scheduling and planning for swimming lessons, soccer practice and birthday parties than we do planning for how to be a living example of what it looks like to live out our child's most fundamental need.

Mom, which do you think your children will most remember when they are adults? Which will be most important to them: The fact that you had a clown at every birthday party, or the fact that they came to know a beautiful life with Jesus because of you?

. . . .

You might be the only "Jesus" your children ever see, so it's critical that you introduce them to God and Christ from the start (if possible). It's important to model the Christlike behavior and establish a strong foundation of faith from an early age so you can equip them to make decisions on their own out of that solid foundation. If you don't accept Christ as your personal Savior until your children are older, it's still important to model the Christlike behavior so that your children can witness the positive change it's made in your life. —Amber Stockton, author

. . . .

The answer is obvious. So let's put more effort into meeting our children's deepest need than we do into meeting needs that are in second, third or even tenth place. Let's show our children what really matters. Our children will watch what we spend our time and effort on. Whatever we spend the most effort on is what they will conclude is most important to us. We don't want to give them the impression that Jesus is a nice accessory to our lives; we want them to know that Jesus *is* our life.

Going Deeper

Do you see like Jesus sees? Ask Him to open your eyes to see what He sees, the way He sees and at the time He sees it.

1 4

Sharing Jesus

"Keep your hands below your shoulders so the baby doesn't get tangled in the umbilical cord."

"Rub Crisco on your belly to avoid stretch marks."

"Don't vacuum. The vibrations are bad for the baby."

You get all kinds of advice when you're pregnant. Some of it is good; some of it is not so good, as in the previous examples (though I wouldn't mind following the advice not to vacuum). The point is, everybody has something to say to a pregnant woman. Every woman loves sharing her hard-earned wisdom, or perhaps wisdom that's been passed down in her family for generations.

You probably won't get a lot of compliments on what people think you're doing right, but even perfect strangers will feel free to tell you when they believe you're doing something wrong.

When I began dating my husband, and when it came time for me to meet his parents, I was nervous. I wondered what my in-laws—especially my mother-in-law—would be like. I don't think I'd ever heard any positive stories about mothers-in-law, but I'd sure heard plenty of negative ones.

My mother-in-law, however, is the kind of mother-in-law everybody wants (thank You, Jesus!). She loves me as well as if I were one of her own flesh-and-blood children. She treats me as well as she treats her son and daughter. She's fun to be with, and I have learned a lot from her. But one of the things I most cherish in our relationship is the way she goes about giving me advice.

She has gotten to know me well enough that she knows when I would welcome advice and when I wouldn't—and she never offers it when I'm not interested. Yet she is always available to give me sound, well-reasoned, godly counsel when I ask for it. She is willing to share her life and her wisdom with me, yet she never does it as if she is superior to me. She offers it from a humble and loving perspective designed to help me.

We younger moms would do well to take a page from my mother-in-law's book when it comes to how we treat each other. Instead of taking sides in the Mommy Wars (breast vs. bottle; working vs. staying at home; homeschool vs. public school; and many more issues), we should focus on building each other up. In other words, we should share Jesus with each other.

What It Means to Share Jesus

Obviously, one of the primary ways we can share Jesus is to introduce Him to moms who don't know Him. We read in 1 Peter 3:15 that we should always be ready to give an answer to anyone who asks us the reason for the hope that we have. It also cautions us to do this with gentleness and respect. In other words, we should talk about Jesus, but we're not to do it with arrogance and condemnation. Gentleness and respect work much better and are more honoring to Jesus anyway.

But sharing Jesus means more than just telling moms about Him. It also means living as He would have lived in the way we relate with others. By acting as Jesus would have related to a mom, we're sharing Jesus with her. In this chapter, we'll look at several ways to share Jesus that are particularly valuable to moms.

Sharing His Kindness

One of my favorite songs in the world is a country song by Trace Adkins titled "You're Gonna Miss This." The theme of the song is how we sometimes wish so much for the future that we fail to realize that someday, we're going to miss what we have now. The last verse of the song describes the kind of day all of us moms have had: there's a plumber working on the water heater, the dog's barking, the phone's ringing, one kid's crying, one kid's screaming. In the official video, the mom is rushing around, frantically trying to deal with everything, and it's obvious that she's apologizing to the plumber for all the craziness. (Sound like any day you've ever had?)

The plumber is probably 20 years older than the mom. He looks like just a regular guy, and he has a kindly face. Upon hearing her apology, he stops his work, smiles reassuringly at her and gently says, "They don't bother me. I've got two babies of my own. One's 36; one's 23. It's hard to believe, but you're gonna miss this." *That* was kindness.

This is a fictional scenario, but scenes like it play out all too often all across the world, every single day. A mom feels overwhelmed. (We've all been there.) She apologizes. (She's frantically trying to make the situation right and calm somehow.) And unlike in the video, she receives a less-than-kind response.

Sometimes, she receives condemnation. *This whole thing is your fault. If you were a better parent . . . if you stayed at home with your kids . . . if you prayed more . . .* And she has to fight off the additional guilt being heaped on her.

• •

When my girls were in middle school and high school, I worried about the things they were faced with and whether they were strong enough to handle the challenges as believers. One of them was faced with a difficult choice and did not make the choice I felt she should have made. Being the drama queen that I was, I went off just knowing I had failed. I had let God down and let my daughter down. As her mother, I had not taught her to handle things. I shared this with an older woman in our church, and she said something I had never thought of before. She told me my daughter was a young woman, not a child. She had to make choices and learn from them. She went on to quote Proverbs 22:6: "Train up a child in the way he should go," and she stopped. I finished, ". . . and when he is old he will not depart from it." This changed the way I handle talking to my girls to this day. God holds them when we cannot. —Susan W.

• •

Often, she receives advice. *Here's what you need to do to fix your problem.* As if the advice giver knows more than the mom does about how she should rear her children. Maybe the advice is good advice. But it's only a Band-aid. It doesn't address the mom's deeper need to know that someone's with her in the struggle.

Other times, a mom might receive a put-down (*What do you expect with so many young kids?*) or apathy, when the responder might say polite things but doesn't really seem to care.

What a mom needs in that situation is Jesus.

She needs His arms around her, whether figuratively or literally. She needs His kindness. She needs to know He cares. She needs to know He's with her in her struggles and overwhelmed feelings.

The Bible tells us that when we show love to others, we make the invisible God visible. So when we love a mom in this situation—when we show her kindness and caring—we make God visible to her. We show her that God cares too. That we're there with her, but that what's more important, so is He.

Sharing His Generosity

I love eating bacon for breakfast. In fact, I would eat bacon every day, all day, if I could. There's nothing better than a good, crispy, salty, flavorful slice of bacon. Mmmmmm.

A few mornings ago, I prepared four such slices of bacon along with some eggs for my breakfast. Glancing around, I realized the kids were nowhere in sight. I quickly set my plate at my place at the table, sat down and prayed.

After the prayer, I opened my eyes to get started on my breakfast, only to find that Jessica had somehow sneaked up right next to me and was standing there smiling confidently at me. Uh-oh. I knew what that meant.

"You want some of my bacon, don't you?" I asked warily.

She nodded, then she looked at me and opened her mouth wide. "Ahhhh," she said, pointing inside her mouth.

I glanced from my cute, sweet little daughter to my precious bacon. Then back to my smiling daughter who stood there hopefully, and back to my precious bacon.

It was a close call. But finally, I picked up one beautiful, crunchy strip. "Here," I said, only half-pretending to be glum. "Have some of Mommy's bacon."

"Thank you!" Jessica said happily. She shoved part of the strip of bacon into her mouth.

Amazing generosity on my part, wasn't it?

Okay, not so much. Yes, I shared my bacon. But I wasn't entirely happy about it.

Fortunately for me, and for you, God never hesitates to be generous to us. He loves to give, and He loves to give to His precious children. He joyfully pours out blessings upon us every day.

He loves to hear us ask Him for blessings. When I heard Jessica ask me for bacon, I wasn't all that thrilled. When God hears us ask Him for something (provided, of course, we're asking from a right heart), He's thrilled. He loves to give, and He never withholds either His time or His resources from us.

When we act like Him—when we give generously to other moms—He is pleased.

There are two primary ways in which we can bless other moms by giving generously as God would: by giving our resources and giving our time.

I'm not talking just about giving money, though there may be times when that's appropriate. I'm talking about things like inviting a friend over for lunch (giving our food); inviting a friend's child along to an activity with our children (giving our money; using our vehicle and gasoline); fixing a friend's computer (giving our knowledge and expertise); or giving a friend things our children have outgrown (giving clothes, toys and books). All of us, no matter what our budget, have some resource to give. Even if it's only letting our friend use our washing machine because hers is broken, that is giving of our resources.

Giving our time can be incredibly helpful and meaningful as well. Babysitting a friend's children probably won't cost us much, if anything, but it might provide her a much-needed break. Making a grocery run for another mom who's home with sick kids won't cost us much—a little gas and some time.

But do you know what? It's not necessarily bad when giving generously costs us something. True, most of us are on a budget, but there will be times when we need to be willing to give sacrificially.

After all, we don't want to teach our children to give only when it's convenient or cheap and easy.

My friend Lori is great at giving. Despite being on a budget, as most of us are, she always has enough extra food to share with others, whether it's invited guests or neighborhood kids that drop in. When I have a need, she's willing to be asked for help at the last minute, and if there's any way she can arrange it, she's glad to help me out. She is generous with her expertise (she's a certified personal trainer) and her love, and she has a remarkable way of making fun for her kids and mine out of ordinary supplies. My kids love going to her home. Why? Because they feel welcome and loved.

That is how God wants us to give. It's how He wants us to illustrate His love to others: by giving willingly and generously.

One final word on sharing Jesus' generosity: Don't always wait until you are asked for something before you give. Look for opportunities to give. When you realize you have something extra, stop and consider whether someone might need that. When you know a friend is in a difficult time in her life, such as after the birth of a baby, when she's going through a divorce or when she's lost her job, look for ways to bless her by giving generously.

After all, God doesn't always wait to be asked before He gives, and that's pretty fortunate for us!

Sharing His Wisdom

When we as moms need advice, whom better to go to than another mom? Especially if she's been in our particular situation before, her advice can be invaluable.

My sister and I are close friends. When her daughter was born, I already had four kids. So, because Kristen figured I had already encountered most of what she would ever encounter, she frequently asked me for advice.

"Breedlove Pediatrics," I would say, answering the phone.

"Grace is making a weird sound," Kristen would say. "I'm going to hold her up to the phone. You tell me what's wrong with her."

I enjoyed being able to give Kristen advice. Kristen is a smart, capable woman with a professional career. But she was a first-time mom. As such, she needed the advice that a more experienced mom could give.

When you give advice like this to another mom, you're sharing Jesus' wisdom. That's because all truth is God's truth, and all wisdom comes from Him. Every fact you know is because God has allowed you to learn it. Every bit of wisdom you have is only what He has granted you. So when you share your wisdom with other moms, you're sharing what Jesus has given you.

There's another way in which you can share His wisdom, and that is to share godly wisdom.

When the question is whether to put your child to bed at 8:30 or 9:00, it's not really a moral issue. But when the question becomes how to discipline your child for back talking you, there are definite moral issues involved.

You, as Christ's representative, have the wonderful opportunity of sharing godly wisdom with other moms. Whether or not that other mom is a Christian, you have the chance to share Christ's principles with her. I'm not suggesting that you try to force a non-Christian mom to convert; conversion is the Holy Spirit's work, not yours. But no matter the other mom's spiritual status, you can still offer godly advice.

Here's what I mean: When a mom—whether Christian or not—wants your advice on how to discipline, you will advise from the perspective that children are to obey and honor their parents, for this pleases the Lord. By encouraging the other mom to require her children to honor her, you will be encouraging her to bring her family in line with principles that will do nothing but honor God and benefit her and her family.

Sharing His Rest

Ahhhhh, sleep, beautiful sleep! I used to know what that was. I remember sleep from oh, say, 10 years ago, before I became pregnant with my first child. Ever since then, restorative sleep has been—well, inconsistent. Just about the time the newest child begins sleeping through the night, his older sister starts wanting to sleep in Mommy and Daddy's bed. And just about the time *that* problem's solved . . . pregnant again! If only I could get eight hours of sleep on a regular basis, maybe even only for a week, I'd be a new person.

But there's another kind of rest that's even more important than physical rest, and that's soul rest. You have the chance to make a huge difference in another mom's life by helping her find soul rest.

Taking vacations, having "mommy time" or even spending a few minutes alone on the porch with a book and a cup of coffee—all these are fun and will bring a measure of rest. So will getting a babysitter or going on a date night, not to mention cutting out extra activities from an overburdened schedule to allow yourself time to relax and just be. Ultimately, if a mom really wants rest, she'll have to come to the end of herself. She'll have to realize that she can't handle everything alone; she needs help. From other moms, sure, but most of all from Jesus.

What kind of help can Jesus give a mom? It all comes from the results of His love for her.

You see, Jesus won't necessarily free up a mom's schedule. He won't necessarily make her circumstances easier. But He can—and will—give her soul peace even in the midst of those circumstances.

You may be able to comfort, counsel, forgive, encourage, rejoice with and give advice to another mom. And remember how we said that the way to make the invisible God visible is to love one another? When you do these things for another mom, when you help give her rest, you are making God visible. Just be sure you credit Him as the one who is truly giving her rest.

• •

I helped a friend one time when she was hosting a baby shower and had her little one-year-old running around at her ankles. She looked completely frazzled, and so I brought the baby back home with me so that she could enjoy the shower without the extra stress. —JoAnna M.

• •

Sharing His Comfort

An old saying goes, Laugh and the world laughs with you; cry and you cry alone.

This saying shouldn't have to come true for any mom. Every one of us needs someone to be with us when we're "crying." We need someone to walk with us through our pain and grief.

One of the best ways you can truly matter in the life of another mom is to minister Jesus' comfort to her. By doing so, you'll show her not only that you care, but that Jesus cares. Let's look at three primary ways you can share Jesus' comfort with another mom.

First, you can grieve with another mom when she is grieving. Many times, when we see someone suffering, our first impulse is to jump in and try to fix the problem or sweep it under the rug. But that never works for long, if at all. A grieving mom doesn't need someone to give her pat answers. She needs someone to come alongside her as she walks through her darkness.

Jesus was willing to grieve with His friends when they grieved. Even though He had all the answers at His disposal, there's not one single instance in Scripture of His giving a pat answer to someone. He never dismissed someone's pain with a wave of His hand as if it didn't matter. In fact, the Gospel of John tells the story of what happened when Jesus' friend Lazarus died. When Jesus arrived on the scene and found people grieving, His heart was moved. The shortest verse in the Bible, which is also one of the most profound, shows Jesus' reaction. It simply reads, "Jesus wept" (John 11:35).

Even knowing He was about to raise Lazarus from the dead, Jesus' heart was still moved at Lazarus' death, and He grieved with those who grieved. We would do well to follow His example. Let people grieve. But be with them in it, and let them see that you care.

A second way to share Jesus' comfort with other moms is to minister to them. Maybe a mom is sick and needs some Jell-O from the supermarket; maybe she is perfectly healthy but needs some help cleaning house; or maybe she needs you to watch her kids while she takes a nap because she was up seven times with the baby last night. In each of these instances you have an opportunity to minister Jesus' comfort to her. In so doing, you show her that you care about her needs and that He does too. And you bring her comfort and maybe even a little more energy or endurance to keep going.

Speaking of which, there is a third way to minister comfort to moms, and that is to be willing to be in it with them for the long haul. Not every situation is wrapped up in 30 minutes, minus commercials. Real-life situations are much messier and usually much longer. Moms who are dealing with long-term situations need someone in it with them until it's resolved, if it ever is.

This is far different from dealing with moms who are unwilling to take steps to help resolve their problems. I'm not suggesting that you allow another mom to manipulate you. What I'm saying is that when a mom faces a long-term, difficult situation and is doing everything she can to deal with it—when she truly wants to get better—you stick with her. By showing her you're with her for the long haul, you can remind her that Jesus cares too, and that He won't ever leave her or forsake her.

The way you treat another mom matters. When you make a difference in her life, you also make a difference in the lives of her children. And when you make a difference in a child's life, you never know whose life you might make a difference in when the child encounters that person later on.

Just being a representative of Jesus matters, moms. Never think it doesn't.

Going Deeper

Tell Jesus you'd love to share Him with other moms. Ask Him to show you ways you can do this.

_____

_____

_____

_____

The Ultimate Reward

I love the Olympics. There's nothing I like better than watching them on TV and cheering for my favorite athletes. The Olympic season is the only time I have the TV on all day, because I happen to think the Olympics are awesome not just to watch but to use as teaching moments for the kids.

Using the Olympics as your basis, you can teach your kids about sports, music, science, culture, history, geography, your native language, foreign languages, character, sportsmanship, math, citizenship, politics and more.

When the Summer Olympics were on four years ago, the kids and I watched them all day long. Our favorite athlete was Michael Phelps. The kids somehow wound up calling him "Uncle" Phelps as a mispronunciation of his first name. Every time he (or any other athlete from the USA) won a gold medal and stood on the podium, we stood on the couch, the coffee table, or any other available surface with our hands over our hearts, pretending we were winning too. ("So you go swimming, then you get a gold medal?" then-five-year-old Ellie asked. "That's kind of how it works for him," I said.)

Olympic athletes work hard—very hard—for years, in order to have a chance to stand atop the podium, see their flag raised higher than the other two and hear their national anthem played for millions of fans. These athletes put forth untold effort in order to have that gold medal placed around their neck as the symbol of their achievement. Every one of them says that all their hard work was worth it in order to gain the prize.

There's a prize for us too, moms. Yes, for all the hard, unglamorous, unrecognized work we do, there is a prize—and it's far greater even than the appreciation from other human beings that we strive for.

I'm not merely talking about the affirmation and thanks we receive from Jesus in this lifetime. You see, as great as that is, He gives those who are faithful to what He has called them something even greater than that.

One day, we will stand before Him and hear Him say, "Well done."

Jesus will look at everything—the glories, the mistakes, the joys, the failures; but most of all, He will look at the fact that you were *faithful*—and He will say, "Well done."

• •

It makes me want to do my best in life because I don't want to disappoint the Father, Son and Holy Spirit who have given so much for me. I pray that I hear His voice every day and can overcome my own stubbornness and be obedient to Him. —Cheryle N.

• •

Let's look at the story of our reward recorded in the book of Matthew:

> "Again, it will be like a man going on a journey, who called his servants and entrusted his property to them. To one he gave five talents of money, to another two talents, and to another one talent, each according to his ability. Then he went on his journey. The man who had received the five talents went at once and put his money to work and gained five more. So also, the one with the two talents gained two more. But the man who had received the one talent went off, dug a hole in the ground and hid his master's money. After a long time the master of those servants returned and settled accounts with them. The man who had received the five talents brought the other five. 'Master,' he said, 'you entrusted me with five talents. See, I have gained five more.' His master replied, 'Well done, good and faithful servant! You have been faithful with a few things; I will put you in charge of many things. Come and share your

master's happiness!' The man with the two talents also came. 'Master,' he said, 'you entrusted me with two talents; see, I have gained two more.' His master replied, 'Well done, good and faithful servant! You have been faithful with a few things; I will put you in charge of many things. Come and share your master's happiness!' " (Matt. 25:14-23, *NIV*)

It didn't matter that Jesus had given one servant more than the other. What mattered was that both of the servants were faithful with what they had been given. No, they weren't perfect; they were human. Despite that fact, at the end, they heard, "Well done," and they were invited to share in their master's happiness.

Isn't it amazing to know that despite everything we've done wrong, if we are faithful to Jesus and to the calling He has given us, we will one day hear that ultimate summary of our work: "Well done"?

Not, "Well, most of it was pretty good, but there were those times when you were impatient, and of course, you remember that time at Wal-Mart when you embarrassed your child in public." But, "Well done."

Why will this affirmation mean so much to us? For two reasons.

First, because of who gives it. The very Person who created us will evaluate our lives and say, "You please Me, your faithfulness pleases Me, and your work pleases Me." Because we are made to find true fulfillment only in Him, His praise will mean more to us than any other.

All the earthly praise we sought or spent time regretting that we didn't have—it will be as nothing in comparison to what we have just received. You see, Jesus' words are not merely a fancy way of saying thank you. They will be a complete evaluation of our lives, and we will be found pleasing. Yes, you—even with all your mistakes and imperfections. Yes, you—even though you felt like most of the time nobody noticed or cared. You have been found pleasing by the one who matters most.

Imagine putting a jigsaw puzzle together. You are almost at the end of the puzzle—only one piece left. You take the piece in your fingers and snap it into position. Your puzzle is complete. You're done. And you are satisfied.

That's how it will be when Jesus gives you that amazing final affirmation. It will be putting the last piece in your soul into place. There will never again be any room to feel unfulfilled. Your appreciation cup will be filled to the brim forever. No more emptiness, ever. *Ever*.

* *

I absolutely love to hear good things about my children! What mother doesn't? Whenever I receive positive comments on my kids' character, I practically glow. If I react that way now, how immensely much more joy will there be for me when Jesus says to me, "Well done." —Linda W.

* *

The second reason this affirmation will be so valuable is this: You can look forward to it with certainty. You don't have to wonder whether or not your unseen faithfulness matters. In fact, it's not unseen. Jesus sees it. And He's prepared to give you the ultimate reward for it—His approval—when you reach heaven.

When you're in the midst of dirty diapers or messy dishes that, frankly, don't do much to fulfill you, remember this: ultimate fulfillment is coming.

When you're on your knees, begging God to show you what to do about your child's misbehavior, remember this: It seems hard now, but approval's coming.

When it feels like what you do doesn't matter or that no one notices or cares, remember this: It matters more than you can possibly imagine. The only one whose approval will fulfill you sees and cares, and He approves. He's just waiting to see you face-to-face so He can say, "Well done."

Amazingly, there's even more to your reward than the final affirmation that will complete your soul forever. There's the invitation to share in Jesus' happiness.

What does that mean? Is that like saying heaven is one giant party?

Well, in a word . . . yes.

Father, Son and Holy Spirit are always completely joyful and satisfied in each other. Their joy spills over to all who inhabit heaven.

When the Lamb (Jesus) receives us as His Bride, there will be a wedding supper to beat all wedding suppers (see Rev. 19:9). I mean, if we as mere human beings have grand and lavish weddings, how much more grand and lavish would a reception thrown by God be?

It already sounds like heaven will be tons of fun. But wait; there's more!

In heaven, there will be no more death, mourning, crying or pain (see Rev. 21:4). There will be the constant presence of a joyful God who takes care of us. There will be incredible beauty—just take a look at Revelation's amazing description of heaven. There will be no more sin, neither ours nor anyone else's.

Is it any wonder God is happy in an incredible place like this? No. What *is* amazing is that He invites us to share it with Him. He gives us the ultimate benediction over our lives by telling us well done, and then He invites us to enjoy His presence in a place so fantastic it puts even our biggest dreams to shame.

That, precious mom, is what you have to look forward to. *That* is your ultimate reward.

Believe it or not, your ultimate reward is not eight hours of restful sleep (though that does sound pretty good to me right now). Your ultimate reward is not getting to take a shower all by yourself or having a day where nobody bickers. Think bigger than that! Your ultimate reward is to be told that you did well and to be invited to spend all eternity with God in the midst of His joyful perfection.

Dream the biggest dreams you can about how you would like to be rewarded for what you do, and know that heaven is far greater than that. Remember, God is able to do abundantly more than all we can ask or imagine, and we can imagine what we think are some pretty big things. So if God can do abundantly more than that—not just a teensy bit more, but *abundantly*—well, then, wow! *That's* a reward I'm going to look forward to!

The Difference Your Reward Makes *Now*

Some days are just plain hard. Some days wear you out. Some days push you beyond what you thought the limits of your endurance were and leave you wondering how much more you can take.

What difference might it make on those days to remember that your ultimate reward is coming? That this life, wonderful as it may be at times, or wearying and discouraging as it may be at others, is not all there is. Heaven is coming. You can be sure of that, because Jesus has promised it.

I bet if we thought about that more often, those exhausting, dispiriting days would get a little easier. Thinking about heaven won't change our circumstances, but it will lift our spirits in the midst of those circumstances. It'll remind us that there's something more to come. Something better.

Maybe it'll even put a smile in our heart or on our face as we get up and go to find out why somebody's screaming in the living room.

Going Deeper

How does it make you feel to know that one day, Jesus will look at your service as a mom and say, "Well done, good and faithful mommy"? Tell Him you can't wait to hear those words from Him, and ask Him to help you continue to be faithful.

1 6

Adjusting Your Perspective

I love it that one of Jesus' favorite miracles (at least, one of the kind that He did most often) was restoring sight to blind people. I can only imagine how difficult it must be to be blind in today's society, and even more so in Jesus' day, when many of the products, programs and services now available to blind people had not yet been invented.

There wasn't really any way to have a job back then if you were blind. Oh, sure, you could probably find something to do, but it wouldn't have made much money. So not only were you blind, but you were considered a non-contributing member of society. Your life didn't count for much except maybe to those who loved you.

Yet Jesus seems to have delighted in restoring sight to blind people, and I bet part of the reason was because He knew He was restoring not only their sight, but also their life. He was opening to them a whole new way to live and become a productive member of society, which, especially if you were a man, was something foundational to your identity.

I imagine the blind man we read about in Mark 8 didn't consider himself to have the greatest life. Until, that is, he and his friends heard that Jesus was in town. Let's look at his story:

> They came to Bethsaida, and some people brought a blind man and begged Jesus to touch him. He took the blind man by the hand and led him outside the village. When he had spit on the man's eyes and put his hands on him, Jesus asked, "Do you see anything?" He looked up and said, "I see people; they look like trees walking around." Once more Jesus put his hands on the man's eyes. Then his eyes were opened, his sight was restored, and he saw everything clearly (Mark 8:22-25, *NIV*).

"Some people"—probably not the man's relatives, or I bet Mark would have written "Some family members"—brought the man to Jesus and begged Jesus to heal him. It doesn't even say that the blind man begged. Maybe he had lost hope; maybe he thought someone like Jesus wouldn't listen to someone like him. In any case, his friends begged Jesus for his healing.

How did Jesus respond? He healed the man—first partially, then completely.

I used to wonder about why He did that. Why didn't Jesus just heal the man outright? After all, He was capable of doing so. It wasn't like He tried and couldn't get it right the first time. Jesus must have had a purpose.

I believe His purpose was to show us that He does, indeed, bring healing, but He doesn't always do so all at once.

For example, you may have been reading this book and felt the Holy Spirit speaking to you, pointing out aspects of His truth that you need to absorb and hide in your heart. You may have thought, *Wow! I never saw it that way before!* as the Spirit illuminated something to your spiritual eyes.

* * *

I will never again feel like God has given up on me or that he isn't taking care of me. I know my relationship with my child is a direct reflection of my relationship with Him. I love that He designed it that way. —Christi B.

* * *

These things are great, and they are absolutely necessary first steps in taking up permanent residence in a new place spiritually. But there are other things that need to happen as well. Let's look at six things that are also part of the process Jesus intends for you.

Acknowledge How You've Reacted When the People in Your Life Don't Fulfill You, and Repent Where Necessary

This might not be pretty. You may find that you have to acknowledge some unpleasant, unattractive and even immature responses.

Some of those responses will also be sinful. For example, when you look at it honestly, you may find that when someone doesn't give you the appreciation you desire, you begin to manipulate him or her into providing it, either through the use of guilt ("Too bad nobody around here is thankful") or by giving the person the silent treatment—silent, that is, except for slamming doors and frequent sighs of irritation and disgust. You may discover that though you never say a manipulative word, you use the look on your face to speak volumes.

If this is the case, or if you have some other favorite but inappropriate response, you need to acknowledge it and repent of it. Saying, "Well, I know I have a problem" but doing nothing about it is worse than useless, because you are then adding the sin of refusing to correct a known wrongdoing.

Mom, be brave. Come clean before God the way you expect your children to come clean to you about their attitudes. Call it what it is. Name specific attitudes and actions that you know were sinful responses. Agree with God that you have been wrong to do these things. Tell Him you're sorry, and ask Him to help you find a new, Christ-honoring response.

Then keep asking. Most of us find it relatively easy to make a change for a little while after we're convicted that we need to do so. Maybe we bridle our tongue the *whole evening*, but then the next morning, after a night of not sleeping well, we're tired, and all of our best intentions disappear when a little hand shakes us awake and a small voice whispers, "Mommy? Can I sweep wif you?" Patience and gentle words go right out the window.

• •

I used to get impatient with the kids when they
were little. I would be inconsistent in discipline and
they would get on my nerves until I screamed
at them. I knew I shouldn't scream at them.
They were babies. —Daphne K.

• •

Keep asking God to help you. It's not like you can only ask once. It's not like you get one chance, and if you blow it, too bad for you. God will accept your repentance and restore you to fellowship with Him as many times as you need it, and He'll help you obey Him any time it's hard. Keep asking. Don't give up when you get it wrong. Don't listen to the devil's voice that hisses, "See? You can't do it." Maybe you didn't do it that time, but God will give you a clean slate to start again. So don't lose hope. Your power to conquer this sin lies in God's greatness, not in yours.

Determine to Let Others Off the Hook for Your Fulfillment

It's good to know that only God alone can fulfill you in the way you need. In fact, it's great! But there's more to being filled with God than just knowing in your head that it's possible. One thing you have to do is make a deliberate decision to let others off the hook for your fulfillment.

If you're like I once was, this thought causes some panic. *Let others off the hook? Are you kidding? If I let them off, they'll never treat me the way they should. I'll be worse off than I am now!*

I know you probably don't want to hear this, as I once didn't, but you need to let them off the hook anyway. Yes, it's possible that when you stop trying to force others to appreciate you "properly," they will do less than they do now. Yes, it's possible that the only thing keeping up a semblance of appreciation is the fact that you are demanding it from them.

But would getting less appreciation from them really be the worst thing in the world?

Now, before you throw this book in the trash, consider one thing: Letting others off the hook of appreciating you makes more room for you to receive Jesus' filling of you. In other words, the less occupied you are with getting your appreciation from others, the more time and emotional energy you will have to pay attention to Jesus, who has promised that He will completely fulfill you. So, yeah, you might lose something in terms of human fulfillment. But you'll gain fulfillment from the Son of God. I hardly think that's a net loss.

Receive Others' Partial Appreciation as a Gift Rather Than a Partial Payment

This one might sound a little weird. It did to me at first, too, when I was just beginning to grasp the concept. But let me explain.

No matter how good someone is at meeting your needs, he or she can only do so partially. That being the case, you have two options: You can regard their appreciation as a gift, or you can look at it as partial payment on what they "owe" you.

Looking at it the first way is kind of like a pleasant surprise. It's like, "Hey! A gift! Great!" Looking at it the second way is like, "Yeah, but where's the rest of it?"

If you've let the person off the hook, as we discussed in the last section, he or she doesn't owe you anything anymore. You're free to accept his or her appreciation as a gift. But if, in your mind, the person is still on the hook, then any appreciation he or she expresses won't mean much to you, because you will be focusing on the fact that he or she didn't do everything you hoped for instead of focusing on the fact that he or she gave you a gift.

Which perspective is going to be more satisfying to you? Do you really think you'll be happier if you keep trying to make sure the other person appreciates you more and more? Or would you be happier being filled by Jesus and receiving the other person's expressions of appreciation as gifts—the "icing on the cake," if you will?

Start Looking to Jesus to Fill You

Let's say you've confessed any sinful responses to a lack of appreciation. You've decided to let others off the hook for appreciating you and to regard any efforts on their part as gifts. That's all well and good. But it will still leave you empty. That's because in order to be filled, you have to look to Jesus.

Jesus promised His disciples that the Father would send the Holy Spirit in Jesus' name to teach them everything and remind them of everything Jesus had said to them (see John 14:26). This is the same Holy Spirit that now lives in you if you have a relationship with Jesus. He will remind you of everything Jesus wants you to know. He will teach you everything you need to know. And this is not just academic information, because when God's truth truly enters your heart, it transforms.

When that happens, you are filled with joy. When the disciples were acting in obedience to God, despite their difficulties, they were filled with joy and the Holy Spirit (see Acts 13:52).

This can be true for you too. Even in the face of a major lack of appreciation, you can be filled with Christ's Spirit and His joy. Not only can you be filled, but you *will* if you seek Him and His fulfillment rather than seeking these things from others.

Are you going to seek appreciation and fulfillment from those who are destined to fail in their efforts, or from the only one who can—and will—do a perfect and complete job?

Begin Performing Your Service to Your Family as Unto the Lord

We've already looked at Colossians 3:23-24 to see that we're commanded to work for the Lord instead of for human beings because it is the Lord who rewards us and it is He whom we serve. That's important to know. But it's also important to know that God guarantees a couple things when you do your work for Him.

First, He promises that your work is never useless (see 1 Cor. 15:58). I don't know about you, but sometimes it certainly seems to me that my work is pretty close to useless. Generally, I get to feeling this way when I've done five loads of laundry and there are still more loads waiting, or when I've made the kids clean up the living room, only to turn around 10 minutes (or 10 seconds) later and find it a mess again.

During those times when I wonder if what I'm doing really matters, I love to remember 1 Corinthians 15:58. My work is *not* useless. Not ever. It *does* matter. It matters even when I can't see it or feel it. I love hanging on to that.

The second thing God guarantees is that He will not overlook your love and efforts toward His saints (see Heb. 6:10). I love knowing that God always sees what I do. It's never invisible to Him. It's never unimportant to Him. It matters, and it's always rewarded.

But that's only if it's done unto Him, desiring to receive *His* reward, rather than done as unto human beings.

· ·

Serving my family has always been something I've enjoyed, because serving is one of my spiritual gifts. I am most fulfilled when I am serving and doing for others. When I was younger, I enjoyed doing all the domestic things required of a homemaker.

I still enjoy doing those things now that I am older, but it is somewhat harder to do them. Just because I have always enjoyed doing those things doesn't mean I have always done them as unto the Lord. When I was younger, I'll have to admit that I went in what would be referred to as "my own strength" much of the time. Now that I am older, I know it was not "my own strength" but strength that God gave me in my youth, because He was and is the source of my strength whether or not I realize it.

I have learned that my attitude about what I have/need to do demonstrates whether or not I am performing the service as unto the Lord. I often pray throughout the day, asking God to help me change my stinking thinking. Also, I need to be sure I am performing the service for His honor and glory and not my own. It's a lifetime of learning. —Elna B.

· ·

Ask God to Plant This Truth in the Deepest Part of Your Heart

We moms desperately need to know that what we do matters. We need to know that we're appreciated. And we need this knowledge to be not merely head knowledge, but heart knowledge as well.

Yet somehow it's difficult for us to absorb this truth. We know it in our heads, but it doesn't make it down to our hearts. We want it to, and we try to force it in there, but nothing seems to work. We still feel unfulfilled, and now it's worse, because we know we don't have to feel that way.

What then is the secret? Simply this: Ask God to plant this truth in the deepest recesses of your heart. Ask Him to fill every crevice in your soul with authentic, life-changing knowledge. Ask Him to do the part He's promised to do, to which you know His answer will be yes. And ask Him to help you do yours—to help you realize when you're beginning to seek your approval from sources that won't satisfy; to make you quick to repent and to return to seeking Him alone; to help you renew your mind (see Rom. 12:2) and replace Satan's lies and temptations to "forget" with God's truth.

You see, God can infuse knowledge into our being in ways we don't fully understand. (That's one reason He's God and we're not.) He can make this knowledge a living, active force in our lives.

All the effort in the world on your part is good, but not if you are doing it apart from God's enabling you to be different. You can't change your heart by yourself; that's why you needed Jesus to save you and why you continue to need Him every day. And just like He did when He saved you, Jesus can transform you from an empty mom, frantically trying to get her needs met by others, to a satisfied mom, filled with Jesus and His Holy Spirit, and more contentment than you ever imagined.

Going Deeper

Tell God you're ready to look to Him for your fulfillment. (If you're not ready, ask Him to help you get to that point.) Thank Him for being willing to fulfill you to overflowing.

Dancing for Jesus

Have you ever had your child stand on your feet, hold onto your hands and lean back and look into your eyes as you danced together?

Have you ever played a CD at a really high volume and danced around the kitchen like crazy until you each got so dizzy and tired you fell over?

Have you ever watched your child do a "happy dance" because she *just couldn't help it*?

If you've done any of these things—or maybe all of them—you know what it is to dance for pure joy.

But have you ever thought about dancing for pure joy out of love for Jesus?

King David did. Well, not for Jesus exactly, but for God. Let's look at the story:

> Now King David was told, "The LORD has blessed the household of Obed-Edom and everything he has, because of the ark of God." So David went down and brought up the ark of God from the house of Obed-Edom to the City of David with rejoicing. When those who were carrying the ark of the LORD had taken six steps, he sacrificed a bull and a fattened calf. David, wearing a linen ephod, danced before the LORD with all his might, while he and the entire house of Israel brought up the ark of the LORD with shouts and the sound of trumpets (2 Sam. 6:12-15, *NIV*).

David is not just *sort of* dancing here. He's not just *kind of* rejoicing. I mean, those people could barely walk six steps before David made another sacrifice and danced some more. He was going all out, giving it everything he had. In fact, he was so filled with joy that he removed most of his clothes so they wouldn't get in his way.

Now, I'm not necessarily suggesting that you start taking your clothes off when you want to celebrate Jesus. (I guess it would depend a whole lot on where you were. For example, church would not be a good place to get mostly naked.) But I *am* suggesting that you and I need to be as enthusiastic about Jesus as David was.

Does that mean that our emotions need to get stirred up all the time? Not necessarily. Those times will come, but not every single day.

Do we have to dance crazy with joy every six steps? Not necessarily. But maybe.

Emotions are fickle and fleeting. What brings us joy one day might make us sad the next, or in different circumstances.

Unless, that is, we're talking about Jesus. When we're crazy in love with Jesus, our natural response will be exuberant joy that can't be contained. I say again that this doesn't necessarily mean we'll elaborately display our emotions, or that our emotions will always remain at a fever pitch. But being in love with Jesus means that, literally or figuratively, we'll stop every so often to dance joyfully with Him.

Maybe not every six steps, but regularly nonetheless.

Being in love with Jesus is like nothing else. You have a great inner peace that only He can give someone about everything, from a simple decision to major life-altering problems. We have a peace about all when we love Jesus. —Michelle T.

We human beings weren't made to be able to live with our emotions at a constantly high level of intensity. But we were made to have those moments when our love overflows so abundantly that we can hardly contain ourselves.

Think about how you felt on your wedding day. Think about the birth or adoption of your first child. *That* kind of joy is what

I'm talking about. The joy that's too big to be contained. The joy that demands spending time in the presence of the loved one. The joy that forces you to express it to the world. The joy that finds indescribable contentment in quiet moments spent alone with your loved one.

You can have those kinds of moments with Jesus.

Not Searching for an Emotional Experience

Just remember that you're not searching for a particular kind of emotional experience, or at least you shouldn't be. You're searching for *Jesus*, and you let the emotional chips fall where they may.

Sometimes you will feel exuberantly joyful in the presence of your Loved One. Sometimes, you may feel quietly content. Those two kinds of experiences look completely different, but both are spiritually nourishing. If you expect your times with Jesus always to look a particular way, you're either going to be disappointed or you're going to try to manufacture a particular kind of experience.

If you are with your Loved One, any exciting emotions you may feel are just icing on the cake. They're sweet, but they're not really necessary, and they're certainly not the cake itself.

Falling in Love with Jesus

To enjoy being in Jesus' presence—to relish it—you have to be in love with Him.

For a long time, I wondered if I really loved Jesus. I *thought* I did. That is, I wanted to. But I wasn't really sure what that was supposed to look like. I began to pray for God to make me madly, passionately in love with Jesus. I wanted love for Jesus to consume me.

I'm not sure I'm there yet. But I do know that I love Him more today than I did yesterday, and that yesterday, I loved Him more than the day before that. I'm progressing. I'm getting there, and I rejoice in that.

How did it come about? As I prepared to write this section, I knew I would have to answer that question. *How* exactly does one grow to love Jesus? How can a mom who wants to be in love with Jesus make it happen?

The answer is simple: You can't make it happen. That is, *you* can't. But *He* can. And He will when you spend time with Him.

· ·

When I just knew about Jesus, when it was all head knowledge, I acted out of obligation and maybe even a little fear. But when I came to know Jesus, when I realized the depth of His love for me, I couldn't help but fall in love with Him. And in loving Him, those things that I used to do out of fear or obligation became a gift, something I wanted to do as an offering to Him. And I found that instead of those things depleting me—leaving me frustrated or worried or even just tired—they gave me fulfillment and joy instead. —Laura T.

· ·

That's all it takes. All you have to do is spend time with Jesus, and you will naturally come to love Him. That's because Jesus is so completely love-worthy, so beautiful and perfect and attractive, that if you come to Him with a sincere heart that desires to love Him better, you won't be able to help it. It will happen. In fact, it's impossible to regularly spend time with Jesus without coming to love Him, if you come with an earnest, seeking heart.

Gradually, over time, you will come to know Him better. And when you come to know Him as He truly is, it's impossible to have any other response than joyful love.

So when you spend time with Jesus, ask Him to open your spiritual eyes. Ask Him to display His awesome love and majesty to you. And be prepared to fall ever deeper in love with Him, from now until the day He calls you home.

Dancing with Jesus

Don't be afraid to "dance with all your might" before the Lord. Maybe you literally dance; maybe you and Jesus spend time together in a different way. Sometimes I sit quietly on my front porch and just talk to Him in my heart; sometimes I drive down the road singing praise songs at the top of my lungs (if you're in the car next to me, don't bother trying to figure out which radio station I'm listening to; it's probably a CD); sometimes I kneel and rest my head in my favorite recliner, and just be with Him.

I don't always literally dance—not with my physical body, that is. But my heart dances.

For me, the phrase from the old song, "Jesus loves me, this I know, for the Bible tells me so" holds incredible personal meaning. And when I think about it, my heart dances.

Another song that makes my heart dance is "Untitled Hymn" by Chris Rice. This song looks at the different kinds of things that can happen to us in life and suggests what our response could be. I love the verse that says,

Oh and when the love spills over and music fills the night;
When you can't contain your joy inside,
Then dance for Jesus, dance for Jesus, dance for Jesus,
And live.

Dance with Him, and dance for Him. We'll look a little more at dancing *for* Him in the next section.

The Audience of One

Imagine something with me for a minute.

Let's say you are a concert pianist. You've practiced piano for years, ever since you could sit on a piano bench. You've put in thousands of hours of study and practice over a period of 20 or 30 years, and now you are accomplished enough to perform in front of sophisticated, paying audiences.

Then one day, you receive an invitation to what promises to be your most important performance ever. Your audience will be superior to any audience before which you've ever played. If you do well, you will receive a phenomenal reward.

You decide to accept the invitation. So you purchase a gown appropriate for such an august performance and you travel to the concert hall. You get dressed. You do your hair. You make sure you look perfect. When the time comes for your performance, you walk confidently onto the stage, expecting to hear the kind of clapping befitting your status.

You hear clapping, all right. But it doesn't sound like there are many people in the concert hall. In fact (you frown and shade your eyes with your hand), it sounds like . . . (you peer past the footlights) . . . there is only one person in the hall.

Sure enough, as your eyes focus on the darkness, you realize there is only one person there. He's on his feet, beaming at you, clapping with all his might, shouting "Bravo!" even before you've played a note.

But he's only one person.

One.

You've traveled all this way, gone to all the effort for . . . *one person?*

In that moment, as you stand peering past the lights, you have a choice. Will you sit down and play, as you've committed to do? Or will you leave the stage in anger and disappointment because that one person isn't worth it?

Precious mom, you perform your motherhood duties before an Audience of One. As the Puritan John Cotton said, everything you do is to be done before God alone, to the glory of Him alone and with a view to pleasing Him alone. Yet too often, we moms decide that an audience of only one isn't worth the time and effort to put into a stellar performance. We want the rest of the seats in the concert hall filled. We want the applause of far more than one. And if we don't get that, we're going to stomp offstage in anger or slink offstage in discouragement.

What we don't realize is that the approval of that one is worth far more than the adulation of millions.

If we're in love with that Audience of One—as we discussed in the previous section—then everything changes! If we're madly, passionately in love with Him, then it really doesn't matter to us whether or not the rest of the seats are filled. Everyone in the world could be clapping for us, but our eyes are still focused on Him because He is our first and greatest love.

• •

It is never enough; man is never really pleased with
another man, because our souls are made to please God. So if
I can please God by just seeking Him, by praying, praising, or
blessing another person, such as my child, it is so much more
satisfying than trying to please man. —Cara B.

• •

Do you see how loving Jesus changes everything? How it is the basis for our entire life? How if we merely respond naturally to seeing Him as He really is—in other words, if we love Him, which we can't help but do—then He is the only one whose praise matters to us, and everybody else's fades into its proper significance, which is to say that it ceases to matter?

We stop noticing how many seats in the concert hall are filled, because we're too busy looking into the eyes of the one who sits front and center.

The one who shouts "Bravo!" before we've played a note.

Going Deeper

Do you dance with Jesus? If not literally, then figuratively? Ask Him to help you fall deeper in love with Him.

18

Encouragement for Single and "Single-ish" Moms

· ·

I [just] need to hear that I'm doing things right,
or even "okay." —Lori H.

· ·

Tania L. met her first husband when she was 23. Both were students in graduate school at the same university. They were immediately attracted to each other and began to date. A year later, they got married.

Everything was fine at first—for several years, in fact. The couple had three children, a boy and two girls. It was shaping up to be the life Tania had always dreamed of.

Then Jim began to drink. When he was drunk, he was abusive both physically and verbally. Tania could never tell whether Jim was going to come home drunk or sober, or whether he was even going to come home at all.

Finally, when the abuse escalated to the point where Tania feared for her children, and Jim was draining their savings account and checking account by purchasing alcohol, so that there wasn't even enough food for the family to eat, Tania filed for divorce.

It's not what she thought would ever happen. When Tania got married, she meant what she had vowed. She assumed that she and Jim would be together forever. But that became impossible, and Tania found herself single, raising two daughters (the couple's son had died in infancy).

Life didn't turn out the way Tania planned.

Jenna V.'s situation wasn't quite as clear-cut. Her husband was never physically abusive, and there was always enough money for food and other necessities. But though Alex never laid a hand on her, he was emotionally abusive. *How long do I stay?* she wondered. *How much of this am I supposed to put up with?* Eight years after getting married, Jenna had had all she could take. She filed for divorce and for sole custody of their children so that Alex wouldn't be able to abuse the children anymore either.

Mary D.'s situation is different. She is married, but her husband's employment keeps him away from home for long stretches at a time. Although her husband is an involved parent when he is home, Mary is essentially a single parent for the majority of the year.

Lori H. is also married. Her husband is in the Army and is deployed for a year or more at a stretch. She, too, is essentially a single parent most of the time. And she is faced with the possibility that her situation might become permanent if her husband does not return alive.

These moms, and many others, face the task of parenting alone most or all of the time. As if being a mom with no father in the picture (at least temporarily) were not enough, these women also feel the pressure to be both mom *and* dad, a situation which Mary D. describes as "unnatural." "The roles are meant for two gender specific types," Mary says. "[After awhile,] it catches up to you."

It's a difficult situation to be in—a situation most women would say they never wanted. "If you're parenting in this situation," says Karen F., "you're likely living a life that is far from what you dreamed it would be. You have to come to terms with broken dreams."

Why It's So Difficult to Be a Single Mom

The obvious issue [is] time and energy (also money). You simply don't have enough. You have to run a tight ship and take good care of yourself. There is no margin for error. None. —Karen F.

I get so caught up in what I should be doing for work, the kids, friends, hubby while he's deployed, and so on, that I forget to take time for me. —Lori H.

I think the most difficult thing is having to be "on" all of the time. If you are sick, too bad. You still have to get the kids taken care of, and you can't just go to sleep to get over your illness. —Tania L.

Ultimately, what makes being a single mom difficult is that there is no one else but you. You are the one who has to make all the decisions; you are the one who has to buy all the groceries and get the oil in the car changed; you are the one who has to give your kids the emotional foundation they need to become happy, healthy adults when they grow up. Being a mom is difficult and consuming enough, but you have to be both mom and dad. You have to do both jobs—or you're afraid your kids will miss out on something vital.

That doesn't leave much time for you. All moms have to sacrifice for their kids, but single moms have to sacrifice even more somehow. They have to find energy when there is none; they have to find extra time when there are only 24 hours in a day. And they have to do it all with what might feel like, as Karen F. said, "no margin for error," because if they don't do it all, who will?

That's an incredible amount of pressure for any mom to be under. But that's not all. Over and over, the moms I interviewed for this chapter admitted they struggle with wondering whether or not they are doing well enough rearing their children since it's essentially all up to them. I asked the question, "Do you ever struggle with wondering if you are doing well enough in rearing your children, since there is essentially only you?" Here are some of their responses:

ALL THE TIME! This is the hardest thing for me. I joke all the time that I'm saving for our children's future therapist bills! I do the best I can, but it often worries me that it's not enough. —Lori H.

All the time. Guilt is a horrible emotion! I try to tell myself that if I am doing my very best then there is nothing to worry about. —Mary D.

All the time, I struggle. I wonder if I should have stayed in a horrible situation for them. . . . I can't afford to give them the things I wish they had (music lessons, more time, vacations). —Jenna V.

It always felt like there was a deficit no matter how much effort I put in. —Tania L.

The guilt can be overwhelming. —Karen F.

True, all moms struggle to a certain extent with wondering if they are doing enough. But for single moms, the struggle can be even more intense, because if they fail to provide something their children need there is no father to take up the slack.

Single moms have to give, give, give—and that's exhausting. Even more so than married moms where the father is often home, single moms can't stop giving, because if they do, they fear their children will suffer. And no mom wants that.

So they always wonder if they're doing enough. Often, they're afraid they're not. The emotional pressure of constantly having to try yet never being sure you're really succeeding—or of being sure you're not—can be overwhelming.

Not to mention the fact that married moms or society in general judge single moms. "There are times when they ask why the father is no longer in the picture," Beth C. says. "It's sometimes disheartening because I don't feel like I [should have] to justify my relationship history to prove my son is well-adjusted."

"I don't know if 'judged' is the right word," Jenna V. says. "I have been passed over for consideration for really interesting things because . . . how can she juggle this if she's a single mom? That hurts. A lot. A whole lot."

Mary D. says, "Despite having a husband, women pity me. They always say, 'I have no idea how you can do it,' or 'Why doesn't he just get another job so that he can be home?'"

Even at church, single moms may feel judged. "As long as I looked 'shiny' at church, being a single mom was all right," Karen F. says. "But in modern American culture, both inside and outside the church, it is seriously not okay to be struggling."

Then there's the internal pressure single moms may feel. "I was mad at myself for not being able to make it work," Tania L. says. "For not choosing a better mate for me, for not being able to have that godly marriage and family I had always hoped for."

Giving without ceasing. Wondering if you're doing enough. Being judged by others and even by yourself. Not having enough time, enough money, enough resources, to give your children what you'd like to give them. Not having the companionship of a spouse.

That's why it's hard. That's why single moms need encouragement, maybe even more so than married moms sometimes.

Precious single or "single-ish" mom, let me tell you this: God sees. He knows. He cares about your struggles. Because He's God? Yes, that. But also because He saw everything a single mom does and struggles with up close.

When Jesus walked this earth, He was reared for a good portion of His upbringing by a single mother.

Mary as a Single Mom

But wait, you say, *what about Joseph? We know Mary had a husband.*

True. But she was probably also single for a good number of Jesus' growing up years—maybe as many as from the time He was 12 until His death.

We know that Jesus' earthly father, Joseph, was alive at least up through the Passover when Jesus was 12. We know this because they all traveled to Jerusalem together (see Luke 2:41-52). But after that, no more mention is made of Joseph. It's pretty significant that Joseph, the head of the household in a patriarchal society, would no longer be mentioned. Is it possible he was still alive and yet all the Gospel writers and the rest of the New Testament writers ignored him? Doubtful.

But there are more clues. When Jesus was dying on the cross, He looked down at His disciple John and His mother, Mary, standing at the foot of His cross, being with Him in the only way they could. Knowing that He was about to die, Jesus said to His mother, "Woman, behold your son!" Then, even more notable for our purposes, He said to John, "Behold your mother!" (John 19:26-27).

There are two reasons this passage suggests that Joseph had died. First, Jesus would not have named John as caretaker for Mary if Joseph had been able. Second, note that Jesus felt it was *His* responsibility to make sure someone cared for Mary. If Joseph were alive, it would have been *Joseph's* responsibility. Yet Jesus knew the responsibility belonged to Him.

A third indication of Joseph's death is that Jesus began His public ministry when He was 30. Jewish tradition said that if a father died, the oldest son was bound to be the man of the house and stay and run the household until he was 30. This could very well have been the reason Jesus began His ministry at that time.

So Mary was a single mother for an unknown period of years. Yes, she had Jesus' help (and wouldn't we all like to have the help of a perfect child who always worked hard and had a good attitude?). But she was still single. She would have known the loneliness of not having a husband for companionship. She would have known the social ramifications of not having a husband in a patriarchal society. She would have had to rear her children on her own. And get this—*she* was rearing the *Son of God*. She, of all people, must have wanted to "get it right."

As the loving, eldest son, Jesus saw Mary's burden up close. He knew what she faced. He saw her joys, her fears, her uncertainties, her loneliness, her inability to provide on her own. He saw how busy she was with several children. He saw all the physical work she did. He saw her on good days and bad days, on days when things were under control and days when things were crazy. And through it all, He loved her and cared for her, not only as her oldest Son, but as her God.

Precious single or sometimes-single mom, this is the way Jesus cares for you too.

He sees your burden. He sees how hard you try. He sees everything you do for "the least of these" despite not having the help you wish you had. He sees how you stretch an insufficient amount of money into a grocery budget that will feed yourself and three kids. He sees how you go without sleep so that you can help your child finish her science project. He sees your loneliness when your married friends get together and don't invite you.

He not only sees, but He *cares*.

And because He cares, because He knows what you are going through, because He knows how stinkin' *hard* it is, He remains by your side, caring for you. No matter whether your spouse left you permanently or has to leave temporarily sometimes—or if you never had a spouse—Jesus will never leave you. Not just because He's God, and He's obligated to stay with you, but because He wants to. He wants to be there to help you bear the burden.

He has a special place in His heart for all moms who are single, just as His own mother was single.

Be encouraged, mom. Jesus loves you. You are special to Him.

Going Deeper

Are you a single mom? If so, have you ever realized what a special place in His heart Jesus has for you? Talk to Him. Tell Him you love Him, and receive His love for you.

19

Encouragement for Moms of Special Needs Children

"Your son has Asperger's."

I had expected the doctor's diagnosis. In fact, my husband and I had taken Kenny to see the doctor in order to get the label we knew was accurate, believing that having such a label would be to his advantage when trying to access therapy services. But knowing the label was coming didn't lessen its impact.

I went home and cried.

Being the mom of a special needs child is hard. It's *very* hard. Not just because of the innumerable doctors, hospitals and therapists; the hours of sitting in hard plastic chairs waiting for the start of an appointment or the end of one; or the times you watch your child cry during therapy because something that comes easily to most children is difficult or terrifying for your child. Not just because of the logistical nightmares involved in planning outings for a time of day when your daughter isn't as likely to freak out, or because of the judgmental stares from strangers in Target when your child's behavior is outside the norm. It's also hard because you love your child, so you grieve for everything your child has lost because of his disability, and you worry about what he might lose in the future.

Will he get married? Will she go to college? Will he be able to hold down a job? Will she have all her physical needs met? Will he have any friends?

These are the questions that trouble the heart of a mom with a special needs child. They are questions that don't have easy answers, but she must try to answer them despite the physical, mental and emotional toll her child's condition exacts from her.

It's hard to come up with profound answers when you're exhausted.

Join the Club

Being a special needs mom isn't a club anyone ever aspires to belong to, yet it's a club with millions of members. Though some moms deliberately choose to adopt these special children, no one would wish special needs upon a child.

That's because we all know that in order to fit in and function in society, you need to stay within certain parameters, which are sometimes narrowly defined.

When our children fall outside those parameters, we become members of a club we wish no one had to join.

Getting Treatment

"The hardest part for us was trying to get a diagnosis," says Jennifer G., "and a correct one at that!"

Sometimes, it's obvious what your child's special needs are called. If your child can't see, it's obvious that he is blind. If she can't hear, she is obviously deaf. But what about if your child looks physically normal until you ask him to throw a football, or she acts "funny," or he doesn't behave "right," or you know that something is "off"? What do you call *that* problem? "It can take years to obtain the diagnosis that best fits your child," Jennifer G. continues.

She's right. I've talked with moms who've spent several years and several thousand dollars trying to find answers or at least a course of treatment that brings some improvement. And even if you do know what your child's difficulty is called, you still may have to explore several different treatment modalities and numerous providers.

An unnamed man whose story appears in Mark 9 understood:

A man in the crowd answered, "Teacher, I brought you my son, who is possessed by a spirit that has robbed him of speech. Whenever it seizes him, it throws him to the ground. He foams at the mouth, gnashes his teeth and becomes rigid. I asked your disciples to drive out the spirit, but they could not." "O unbelieving generation," Jesus replied, "how long shall I stay with you? How long shall I put up with you? Bring the boy to me." So they brought him. When the spirit saw Jesus, it immediately threw the boy into a convulsion. He fell to the ground and rolled around, foaming at the mouth. Jesus asked the boy's father, "How long has he been like this?" "From childhood," he answered. "It has often thrown him into fire or water to kill him. But if you can do anything, take pity on us and help us." " 'If you can'?" said Jesus. "Everything is possible for him who believes." Immediately the boy's father exclaimed, "I do believe; help me overcome my unbelief!" (Mark 9:17-24, *NIV*)

The analogy falls a little short, because I am NOT comparing having a special need to being possessed by a demon. What I want us to look at is how similar we as moms sometimes are to the father in this story.

This father had been trying for so long that he didn't even know whether it was possible for his son to be helped. Yet he continued to seek help because he had to. This was his *son*, after all.

I remember a time when Kenny was receiving treatment three times per week. At least once each week I would have to load not only him but also our other three children into our minivan and drive to therapy. While Kenny participated in his group, the three girls and I would sit in the lobby and wait. I brought various different activities to try to keep the girls from getting too bored, but it was hard. They didn't like being there. I didn't like having to keep them entertained there. I dreaded each session.

And then I found out I was pregnant with Baby #5.

Juggling Needs

So whose needs get prioritized? Kenny's, for therapy? Mine, for rest during an exhausting pregnancy? My three "normal" children's, for time spent focusing on them instead of on their brother?

"I sometimes feel bad for [my daughter] because some decisions in our family are based on what's best for [her brother]," says Martha S. "I'm concerned she may feel he is more important than she is, so I try to make sure I make some concessions for her too, and that often leaves me stressed and worn out."

Becky W. says, "For the oldest child, it felt like life revolved around my son. For the most part, that was true. Doctor's appointments, therapy, discipline and extra time spent with him. She has grown to be more compassionate toward him and protective even, but it was tough when we first started having problems, because she thought we treated her differently."

As the mom of a special needs child, not only do you have to take care of one child's special needs, but you also have to take care of the needs of your other children. You don't want any of your children to suffer or to think they are less loved or valued. It's a tough balancing act, because you don't want to help one child at the expense of another, and sometimes it seems like that's what's happening.

Doing the Right Thing

I've never yet met a mom who says, "I never wonder whether I'm doing the right thing for my child." We all wonder sometimes, even if our child has no special needs. But moms of special needs children wonder—or worry—even more. It's hard enough to know what a typical child needs. How do you make sure you're doing the right thing for a child who's not typical?

One question I asked several moms of special needs children was, "Do you ever wonder if you are doing the right thing (discipline, therapies, and so on) for your child?" Over and over, the response was, "ALWAYS!!" (Note the capital letters and extra exclamation mark these moms used.)

"Every day. All of the time. Not a day goes by [when I don't wonder]," says Crystal S. "We do all we can, but it isn't enough. I feel like I should always be researching, reading, working with him and never, ever resting."

"YES! I am constantly questioning how I discipline him," says Heather W.

Martha S. says, "ALWAYS!!! I always feel like I'm missing something, that I haven't been told about a certain therapy or that we're not getting all the services we need because insurance won't take care of it."

Jenna V. makes a good point. "A better question may be, Do I ever NOT wonder about this?"

Long-term uncertainty coupled with the intense pressure to "get it right" often leaves special needs moms drained, confused, frustrated, and sad.

But we keep going. Why? Because we have to.

You Keep Going

"As a single mom with a special needs child," says Martha S., "it's hard to find someone who will watch him for me where I don't feel like they will regret it because he is unable to control his behavior. . . . As a consequence, [I] get no ME time."

Over and over, the special needs moms I interviewed talked about needing "me" time but having difficulty getting any due to the impossibility of finding someone who can cope with their special needs child. All moms need time to themselves, but moms of special needs kids can experience this need to a greater degree. We often have to be even more intensely involved with our children than do moms of children without special needs, whether by taking them to appointments, trying to help them make progress, or simply relating to them.

How do you keep going when you feel utterly depleted? How do you continue to put one foot in front of the other when there is no end in sight, and due to the nature of your child's disability, there may never be? How do you go on when you just . . . *can't*?

Maybe you live near a church with a program that ministers to special needs families. Maybe you have understanding friends or a spouse who's willing to pitch in. But even if you do enjoy these significant blessings, there's still one more you need, which happens to be the most important one of all. Fortunately, it's available to you no matter what your child's needs are or where you live.

Your Biggest Support

We all know that as moms, we need God. We know that we need to operate in His strength and run to Him with our damaged or worn-out emotions. But when you're dealing with the turbulence caused by having a special needs child, "Just take it to God" sounds like nothing more than a pat answer, and we (rightly) despise those.

Let me tell you why it's not a pat answer. Let me share with you the neat realization God brought me to just recently that puts it all into perspective and makes running to God seem like a great first option instead of something to do because there's no other hope.

That realization is this: Our God is not a one-size-fits-all God. By this I mean that He relates to each of us individually and perfectly. He doesn't have only one way of relating that might not cut it for some people. No, He gives each person what she needs. That means that God stands ready to give you even more in some ways than He gives your friends with what society would call "normal" children. In other words, you don't have to try to get by on a portion that's meant for someone with children who don't have the issues yours do. There is more available to you.

When you crawl into God's lap or collapse exhausted on the floor at His feet and pour out your need, God doesn't dispense a standard-sized portion of comfort with which you have to be content. He offers you comfort, compassion and support in proportion to your need.

That means, precious special needs mom, that there is *a whole lot* available to you.

You need an extra dose of wisdom as you try to ensure that your child receives the best treatment or therapies. You need an extra portion of comfort when people give you "that look" in the grocery store because your child is having a meltdown in the middle of the cereal aisle, and you know there's really not a lot you can do about it right at the moment. You need an extra supply of friendship when other moms don't invite you and your children places because they don't know how to include your special needs child—or don't want to. You need an extra measure of rest when you've given every last thing you have to give, and you're exhausted; of understanding when no other human being really "gets it" why you have it so hard; of compassion when you have to watch your child suffer because of other children's ignorance or cruelty; of hope when you wonder how your child's disability will affect him in the future.

Those extras are what God freely makes available to you.

How does He make it work? I don't know exactly. But He does. He knows exactly how to minister to your spirit, mind and emotions so that you are restored and refreshed. Never forget that He is the God who can do "far more abundantly than all that we ask or think" (Eph. 3:20). And that's what He wants to do for you. He wants to provide for you commensurate with the need He has woven into your life.

A Word About Your Child

So yes, you have a burden to bear—all the things associated with having a special needs child. (The child him- or herself is never the burden.) And yes, God is ready, willing and able to meet your needs beyond what you can imagine.

But that's not the only encouragement He offers you. In fact, it may not even be the biggest.

When Kenny was about three years old, his difficulties were much more pronounced. One of his most significant difficulties was with speech. He could recite lots of information, but he didn't know how to use speech to connect with other people. For example, if you called his name, he would look at you because he knew that when you said "Kenny" you meant him. But if you asked him, "What's your name?" he wouldn't respond, because he didn't understand the question. He didn't know what information you were trying to elicit.

When I prayed for him, I often begged God to help him with his speech. Beseeching? Yep, I did that. Then I would continue on to pray for Lindsey, my next child.

One particular morning when I asked God to help Kenny with his speech, something different happened. God spoke to me, Spirit to spirit, and said, so clearly that I still remember His exact words today, "The greatest work I do in your son will not be in the area of his speech."

That stopped me. I had been praying regularly for Kenny to be able to talk better. By His response, God assured me that He would indeed help Kenny in this area. But God's answer also made me realize that I had been thinking too small. I had been thinking "speech" when God had far bigger designs in mind for Kenny's life.

That's the word I want to leave you with, precious mom of a precious special needs child. Your child is valuable to God just as he or she is. He won't become more valuable when he finally learns to talk better. She won't become more important to God when she is able to walk without crutches. He wouldn't be more precious to God if he didn't have those scars.

Your child is wholly beloved by God just as he or she is, completely useful to God just as he or she is and fully acceptable to God. Just as he or she is. And even if God should choose to heal your child in one miraculous moment, *that* would not be the greatest work that God did in your child's life. God has already done the incredibly awesome work of creating your child, and He is pleased.

Not that He rejoices at disability and pain. He doesn't. But He rejoices that your child, just as he or she is, reflects the majesty of His creation. Never think that because your child has some characteristic that society might term "undesirable" that he or she is undesirable to God. Nothing could be further from the truth.

In fact, when God sent His own Son into the world, He gave Him a body that didn't meet society's standards either. We read, "He had no beauty or majesty to attract us to him, nothing in his appearance that we should desire him" (Isa. 53:2, *NIV*). It doesn't say, "He had *a little* beauty." It says He had *no* beauty. Jesus was nothing special to look at by any stretch of the imagination. Nobody looked at Him and was impressed.

Your child may have some aspect of him- or herself that isn't "much to look at" either. Society may not be impressed. But God is. He is fully in love with your child no matter what society thinks. In terms of His decision to love your child, He doesn't care whether your child can walk well, behave politely or look pretty or handsome. It doesn't bother Him that your child needs a wheelchair or can't tolerate fluorescent lighting.

The greatest work He does in your child won't be in the area of your child's disability. His greatest work in your child was creating your child to be completely lovable and acceptable as far as He is concerned, and in developing a plan for your child's life that He considers worthwhile, even if others don't see it.

Be encouraged, precious mom.

Your child matters to God. Just as he or she is.

Going Deeper

Talk to God about your child. Thank Him for giving you this child and talk to Him about the parenting struggles you face. Ask Him to minister to your heart exactly what you need right now.

_____

_____

_____

_____

_____

_____

_____

_____

_____

Encouragement for Moms
Who Had a Difficult Childhood

Let's face it: not many moms had the kind of childhood we see portrayed on TV shows like *Leave It to Beaver* or *The Cosby Show*. Very few moms, if any, had a childhood so perfect. But for some of us, our childhoods didn't even come close.

"The running theme of my childhood was pain," Carrie T. says. "I was my mother's punching bag for 20 years. She used to leave me when I was very young. When I was three, I was placed in the care of an aunt . . . and then she decided she wanted me back again. So she married a man and had three more kids. I continued to be the target of all of her anger. I watched her treat my brothers and my sister kindly while she screamed at me and beat me. She did things like make me sit at the dinner table and watch the family eat, and I wouldn't be allowed to. I found out when I was 10 that her first husband wasn't my father. I found out because I told her I didn't want to be with her, that I wanted my daddy, and she told me he didn't want me because I wasn't his."

As I read Carrie's words, I cried for that little girl sitting at the table watching everybody else eat.

Different Stories

Each mom I spoke with for this chapter had a different story. Some told of horrific physical or sexual abuse. Some told of equally damaging emotional abuse. All of these women told, even if not in so many words, of feeling unloved. Unvalued. And sometimes (even often), afraid. A common theme in almost every story was, as Becky W. wrote, "Our household was ruled by chaos, inconsistency, yelling, criticism, harsh punishment and no healthy boundaries." I can identify with many of these feelings because my childhood was difficult too.

What happens when a mom who grew up in a home like that becomes a mom herself? How do her experiences affect her parenting?

Trying Not to Repeat Mistakes

Without exception, each mom expressed concern, whether present or past, over whether or not she would be able to provide her children the loving, secure home she never had. Fawn T. wrote, "My parents were both selfish. They did what they wanted, and my wants were last. I was well cared for and provided for, but emotionally I was starved. I hope that my selfishness does not affect my children in the same way."

Heather H. wrote, "I don't know what I'm doing. Having never had a good example of a Christian family, I often feel like I'm in over my head. I don't know how to be the mom that my kids need."

It's hard to give what you haven't received. And many of us who grew up in difficult or abusive homes never saw a good example up close from any other family either. Heather H. continues, "I never knew what a real family should look like or how they acted. What kind of things they did when no one else was around."

Cheryl M. writes, "I did parent [the way my own parents parented me]. And when I saw it, my oldest daughter was four or five. I wept for days, feeling that I had set her up to be crippled like me. It was agonizing days and weeks of crying out to God to show me how to do it differently."

Days, weeks, months and even years of crying out to God, begging Him to help us do it *right*, so that we don't wound our children, causing them the same deep and lasting pain we experienced. Living in constant fear that we're not giving our children what they need and that they'll suffer because of us in ways we understand all too well.

Even if the fear isn't constant, it often resurfaces, especially when we make a parenting mistake. Remember the incident I told you about where I yelled at Ellie for no good reason? I apologized over and over, but I wondered, what had I just done? And almost all the moms I talked with struggled with wondering just how bad their parenting mistakes were.

Living with Uncertainty and Fear

Moms who have had a difficult childhood not only live with the pain of whatever happened (or failed to happen) but also wrestle with uncertainty and fear.

We wrestle with uncertainty because we don't know what a healthy family is really supposed to look like. Sure, we may have read books about healthy families, Christian families, or both. We understand principles such as "Members of a healthy family should show love to each other" or "In a healthy family, there is room for disagreement." But we don't know how to put these principles into action.

It's like when you're learning a foreign language. It's easy to understand that yes, there are certain grammar principles. This verb has these endings. Prepositions only occur in certain places. It's applying those principles all at the same time and coming up with a complete, grammatically correct sentence that's the tough part.

We wrestle with fear because while we know how a child who feels insecure and unloved would respond to certain mistakes, we don't really know how a child with a secure foundation would respond. Is the mistake we just made bad enough to cause a wound? Or is it something our child will just shake off and move on with no ill effects? (And how is that even possible, anyway?)

We want so badly to parent in a way that will show our children they are loved and valued; that will provide a secure foundation for our children's emotional and physical future; and even, if possible, that will cause our children one day to say, "Mom did a great job. I want to parent as well as she did."

Parenting Well

Parenting well involves providing love and security for our children. It means showing them they are valued and wanted. It means delighting in them instead of showing by our actions or tone of voice that they are a burden. It means putting their needs before our own. And did I mention that it means love, love, love?

It's easy to feel like parenting this way is an impossible task, whether because we've never seen it in action or because we don't believe we have the skills or knowledge ourselves. And it's frustrating and grieving when we live our lives never sure if we can succeed at what we want most to do.

Precious mom whose childhood was hard, let me assure you of something that God taught me in my struggle: It *is* possible for you to parent well. And you are *going* to make mistakes.

How can these ideas both be true? How can we consider ourselves a good parent if we know we're going to mess up?

First, we need to realize that only God can be perfect. We're not God. Therefore, we're not perfect. Seems obvious, right? But too often, we moms whose parents failed us get the idea that only by being perfectly loving, perfectly patient, and so on, can we be what our children need.

Friend, let me tell you that is a lie straight from Satan. *You* can be a good parent—even a great parent. Yes, there are things you need to stop doing or start doing, but that is always true for every mom, no matter what kind of childhood she had. It's true simply because she is a human being. Granted, moms who had a difficult childhood may have more challenges when they start out. But guess what? We have the same amazing God as moms who had a near-perfect childhood.

I hope you're getting excited with me, because here's why that matters so much: With *every single mom on this planet*, God has to fill in the gaps between her imperfections and the kind of parenting He wants children to receive. That's with *every single mom*. *All* moms have areas where they need God's help. *All* moms need God to meet their children's needs in ways they cannot. So the fact that you need this too is nothing against you. After all, you didn't choose your childhood, and if you could have, you would have chosen much differently. It doesn't mean your children are doomed to suffer as you did. It simply means you're human, and you need God to help you.

If you want to be a great mom, you don't have to be perfect. All you have to do is seek God, listen to His voice and take action where He tells you to. And *that's* a whole lot easier than attempting perfection.

Being Parented

Dealing with parenting struggles isn't the only issue moms who had a difficult childhood face. Sometimes we think that if we just knew we were doing a good enough job we would be content. We forget that there are areas in which we still need healing. We forget that we still need to be lovingly parented ourselves.

It seems like every time I get to thinking that I've finished healing, I become aware of another area in which I need to heal more fully. This was especially true after I became a parent myself. As I parented my daughter and did certain things for her, old issues arose. Each time this happened, I would find myself getting angry, resentful and sad. I had to work through the issues and emotions, asking God to heal me even more deeply. It was like peeling back the layers of an onion. When one thing got taken care of, another thing was exposed.

Gradually, I became aware of another emotion too: grief. Grief that I never had and will never have the parenting I desired. That's because my parents don't believe there were any significant problems with the way they parented. My perspective is different. And I am doing my best to mother well in spite of it.

For many years, I searched for the love and security I wished I had received from my parents. I remember a time when I sought counsel from a Christian leader I respected. During our session, he said, "If you only remember one thing from this session, remember this: God is not the reflection of your earthly father. He is the *perfection* of your earthly father." He went on to explain that everything I had ever wished my father or mother to be, God was that times a billion.

That idea proved to be a major factor in my healing.

We can all imagine how we would have liked our parents to act. If it were up to us, they would have been kind and loving. They would have put our needs before their own. They would have been understanding, encouraging and firm but not harsh. They would have stuck around and never left.

All those things that we can imagine, God is, but magnified. And that's the kind of parenting that's available to us now, if we will accept it from Him. Too often, we don't come to God because we know He's supposed to be our heavenly Father, and we don't want another parent like the ones we had on earth. But God isn't like our earthly parents. He isn't even like the best earthly parents. Even the best are but dim reflections of how amazing a Parent God is.

Maybe we who had difficult childhoods can imagine a little better what God is like because we have spent more time longing for what we hoped to receive. And maybe, just maybe, we're even more grateful for God's wonderful qualities because we know the alternative. Those two things set us up for an amazing, incredible relationship with the Lover of our souls. If we will just come to Him, we can receive everything we ever hoped for.

Maybe we've tried to come to Him in the past and haven't felt that we received. Maybe that's part of our difficulty in coming to Him now. Or maybe we simply don't comprehend the reality of a parent who loves us so perfectly and so much. But if we will just come and put aside any lie of Satan that says we can't come, or that we shouldn't because we don't deserve to, or that God will only let us down like everybody else, we will find love and healing beyond our wildest dreams. Never forget that God is the God who can do abundantly more than all we ask or imagine (see Eph. 3:20).

That applies to loving us and healing us. So, precious mom, no matter where you are in your struggles to heal, if you will just come to Him and let Him wrap His arms around you and parent you in the only way it is possible for Him to parent, you'll have what you've always wanted. You'll have a loving parent who completely meets your every need. A parent who's always there for you. A parent who will never abuse you or neglect you or make you feel like He doesn't want you. A parent who loved you so much that He sent His Son to die on the cross for you so that He could pull you close and love you.

I admit that I'm still learning what this is like. (Because we've learned not to trust anyone, it can be hard to trust God.) But I'm getting there. As God proves Himself trustworthy again and again and again, I'm learning to have confidence in Him. I'm learning that the security I always longed for is real, but it's found in a different Person from whom I thought it should be found. As I learn, the layers of my heart heal, and I become more and more the person I was always meant to be.

This can be your experience too. It won't be immediate. Though it can take only an instant to be wounded, it takes time to heal. But healing *will* come if you stay close to the Source of healing. It *will* come. And you'll begin to understand, really and truly understand, what it is to be deeply and fully loved.

Come to Him. Let Him love you in the way you've always longed for. It can start right now.

Going Deeper

If you're afraid of coming close to God, or you don't know how, just tell Him that. He'll help you. Ask Him to pour down His love upon you and reveal Himself to you as the Parent you've always wanted and the Lover of your soul. Then ask Him to help you reflect His love to your children.

Conclusion

"Jesus loves me, this I know . . ."

We talked about that song in chapter 5, where we remembered (or maybe learned for the first time) how much God loves us. Now, at the end of the book, we come back to that point.

Why? Ultimately, that's where the whole message of this book—and the message of the gospel—comes back to.

Jesus loves me. It's like when Jesus was asked which was the first and greatest commandment. He answered that the first was to love the Lord your God with all your heart, soul, mind and strength, and the second was like it: Love your neighbor as yourself. He said that every part of Scripture ultimately comes back to these two ideas (see Matt. 22:39-40).

Likewise, the foundation for our entire lives as moms, as women, and even as people is laid upon the fact that Jesus loves us.

Jesus loves us; therefore, we are loved beyond measure and never need to feel unloved ever again.

Jesus loves us; therefore, what we do matters, because He has called us to something that is valuable to Him. We never need to feel insignificant ever again.

Jesus loves us; therefore, we are appreciated by the one whose affirmation matters most. We never need to feel unappreciated ever again.

Jesus loves us; therefore, He will heal us (though He gets to choose the way and the time to make this happen). We never need to feel broken beyond repair ever again.

Jesus loves us; therefore, He took the punishment for our sins that we deserved so that we wouldn't have to take it. We never need to feel hopeless ever again.

Jesus loves us; therefore, He made it possible for us to be friends with God instead of enemies. We never need to feel insecure or unwanted ever again.

Jesus loves us; therefore, He fills our emptiness with His Spirit, which is far better than anything we might attempt to fill ourselves with. We never need to feel empty ever again.

Ultimately, it all comes back to Jesus' love for us. And if we ever truly get to know Him, we will love Him too. We won't be able to help it (not that we would want to).

Why does this matter so much? If you get one thing from this book, I hope and pray that it's a deeper, stronger, more loving relationship with Jesus. That's why I write: to glorify Him and make Him known, so that every mom who reads about Him can realize not only what He's done for her but also how wonderful He is, so that she'll naturally come to love Him more.

I hope you've seen Him in these pages and come to know Him a little bit better. I pray you've heard the one who loves you more than anybody here on earth possibly could, speaking to your heart.

He wants you to know that you matter, mom, and that you're loved. You matter to your family, and they love you, whether or not they always show it. You matter to society, whether or not society truly appreciates you. You matter to your friends, and you matter to me. But most of all, you matter to Jesus.

If you still can't quite grasp this marvelous fact, that's okay. I can't either. None of us truly does. In fact, we'll spend all eternity in heaven learning more about His incredible love and rejoicing in it. But if you need someone to help you figure some of this Jesus stuff out, please don't hesitate to contact me through my website. I'd love to walk alongside you in your journey to know Jesus better.

May I close with a prayer for you?

Precious Jesus,

I pray for the mom reading these words right now, that she will continue to hear You speaking to her heart. I ask You to plant deep within her heart the desire to know and love You and the knowledge that she is deeply loved and valued by You. You have called her to be a mom, which is a beautiful and prized calling. Strengthen her in her efforts to serve her family. Give her patience when she needs it; sleep when she's tired; and endurance when she doesn't feel able to continue. Most of all, Jesus, I ask you to grant her a closer relationship with You, the source of all life and goodness. Draw close to this precious mom and let her feel Your presence. May she always know Your love.

In Your name, Jesus. Amen.

About the Author

Megan Breedlove is the author of numerous devotionals and articles, both online and in print. With a heart for encouraging moms, Megan is a popular speaker at churches and women's groups. She graduated from Baylor University with a University Scholars degree (with an emphasis in psychology and foreign languages) and from Southwestern Baptist Theological Seminary with dual master's degrees in Marriage and Family Counseling and Religious Education. Megan and her husband, Phillip, reside in Fort Worth, Texas, with their five children, Ellie, 10; Kenny, 8; Lindsey, 7; Jessica, 5; and Timmy, 1. They attend Southfield Christian Fellowship in Arlington. Megan enjoys reading, racquetball, playing the piano, and studying foreign languages. To contact Megan, or to read her weekly uplifting devotionals, visit her website at www.MannaForMoms.com.

• •

To contact the author, please visit the following:
Website: www.mannaformoms.com
Email: megan.breedlove@mannaformoms.com
Facebook: http://www.facebook.com/pages/
Megan-Breedlove/123825034311589
Twitter: http://twitter.com/MeganBreedlove

God, in His infinite mercy, has called me to encourage moms to glorify and enjoy Him in their daily lives. If your church or mother's group would like to receive that ministry through a personal visit, please contact me. I'd love to speak to your group in person.

I do not charge a "speaker's fee" as such. My husband and I believe that God's desire for us is to make His encouragement available to all, regardless of ability to pay. If a group is able to contribute toward my expenses, we ask them to do so. However, we don't want finances to prevent a group from requesting God's encouragement through me.

Therefore, if you would like for me to come speak to your group, I request that you pray for the following things:

- That God will clearly reveal to you, to me, and to my husband whether it is His desire for me to speak to your group;

- That God will provide for my travel, lodging, and child-care needs, whether through your organization or in some other way;

- That I will be faithful to hear and to clearly communicate the message that God wants me to deliver to your group; and

- That your hearts will be prepared to hear God's mind and heart speaking to yours.

On my website are some possible topics for me to address with your group. However, with advance notice, I can also prepare to speak on a topic you request.

I look forward to meeting you and your group!

God Is in Every Hilarious, Exhausting, Heartwarming Mommy Moment!

Manna for Moms
ISBN 978-0-8307-5763-3
ISBN 0-8307-5763-5

Between diaper changes, carpools, meals and spills, is it possible to find quality time with God? If only you could connect with your Creator and vacuum cereal out of the car seat at the same time! Megan Breedlove, a stay-at-home mom of four energetic little ones, has discovered the secret: Recognize that He is there in every messy, miraculous moment. *Manna for Moms* is a one-mom-to-another devotional that will inspire you to look up and lighten up—even when you're cleaning up! Each devotion provides encouragement and inspiration to help you face every hectic day with an open heart, expecting God to reveal Himself in the midst of whatever chaos arises! Megan also offers tips and suggestions for staying tuned in to God's presence in your interactions with your kids. Instead of struggling to find time with God, share your hair-raising mothering adventure with your loving heavenly Father.